AF269646

# The Spiritual Marriage between Christ and His Church and Every One of the Faithful

# The Spiritual Marriage between Christ and His Church and Every One of the Faithful

Girolamo Zanchi

Translated and introduced
by Patrick J. O'Banion

**REFORMATION HERITAGE BOOKS**
Grand Rapids, Michigan

*The Spiritual Marriage between Christ and His Church and Every One of the Faithful*
© 2021 by Patrick J. O'Banion

All rights reserved. No part of this book may be used or reproduced in any manner whatsoever without written permission except in the case of brief quotations embodied in critical articles and reviews. Direct your requests to the publisher at the following addresses:

**Reformation Heritage Books**
3070 29th St. SE
Grand Rapids, MI 49512
616-977-0889
orders@heritagebooks.org
www.heritagebooks.org

*Printed in the United States of America*
21 22 23 24 25 26/10 9 8 7 6 5 4 3 2 1

---

Library of Congress Cataloging-in-Publication Data

Names: Zanchi, Girolamo, 1516-1590, author. | O'Banion, Patrick J., 1975-
    translator.
Title: The spiritual marriage between Christ and his church and every one of the
    faithful / Girolamo Zanchi ; translated and introduced by Patrick O'Banion.
Other titles: Spirituali inter Christum et ecclesiam singulosque fideles, connubio,
    liber unus. English
Description: Grand Rapids, Michigan : Reformation Heritage Books, [2021] |
    Includes bibliographical references and index.
Identifiers: LCCN 2021028203 (print) | LCCN 2021028204 (ebook) | ISBN
    9781601789044 (hardcover) | ISBN 9781601789051 (epub)
Subjects: LCSH: Mystical union—Early works to 1800. | Marriage—Religious
    aspects—Christianity—Early works to 1800. | Jesus Christ—Mystical
    body—Early works to 1800.
Classification: LCC BT767.7 .Z3613 2021 (print) | LCC BT767.7 (ebook) |
    DDC 201/.7—dc23
LC record available at https://lccn.loc.gov/2021028203
LC ebook record available at https://lccn.loc.gov/2021028204

---

*For additional Reformed literature, request a free book list from Reformation Heritage Books at the above regular or email address.*

*For Isabel*

# Contents

# Preface

The origins of this translation date back more than two decades to my studies in historical theology at Westminster Seminary California, where I first encountered Girolamo Zanchi. To be honest, I think that he initially intrigued me because the notion of a Protestant Reformer with an Italian name seemed so peculiar and unexpected. The deeper I dug, the more intrigued I became, and I soon realized that I had not only stumbled across a fascinating and significant historical figure but also struck upon a rich vein of theological reflection and piety. Unfortunately, at the time I could only access Zanchi's massive corpus by way of a microfilm reader. Subsequent digitization projects brought his works to the Internet but, even so, they were not particularly readable. Even for the handful of writings that had been translated into sixteenth-century English, early modern orthography, prose style, and typography conspired with semantic shifts to deter all but the most intrepid literary explorers.

My primary motivation for bringing *Spiritual Marriage* to press is the hope that it will encourage readers to meditate on what it means to be united with Christ so that they might learn to love the church's Bridegroom more deeply and express that love by living "soberly, righteously, and godly in the present age" (Titus 2:12). My secondary motivation is to make Zanchi better known. The last three decades have seen more scholarship produced on the Italian than the previous three centuries combined, but virtually all of it is found in scholarly journals, doctoral dissertations, and academic monographs. Only those with lending privileges at a good research library or an expansive personal budget for books can lay hold of such resources. And, of course, for those without Latin, almost all of Zanchi's writings remain out of reach.

I hope this new English translation of *Spiritual Marriage*, which seeks to be true to the original while being readable (and perhaps even pleasant), will be a small first step toward making Zanchi and his work better known and more accessible to a wider audience. It was made primarily using the 1591 Herborn edition published by Christopher Corvinus as *De spirituali inter Christum et ecclesiam singulosque fideles, connubio, liber unus*. It was not made on the basis of a critical edition of the Latin text and does not seek to account for textual variations, but comparisons were made with other Latin editions, as well as with the older English (1592) and the French (1594) translations.

Bringing any work from one language into another is a complex endeavor, and several idiosyncrasies of the original treatise and this translation of it should be noted. First, Zanchi quotes Scripture in ways that were typical for his contemporaries but that may be a challenge to modern readers. He frequently inserts parenthetical glosses and interpretations in the midst of a Scripture quotation. In this translation, those interpolations are enclosed in parentheses. Furthermore, his quotations of Scripture are often elliptical, meaning he only gives a small portion of a larger text; paraphrastic, meaning he offers the gist of a passage without seeking to reproduce it word for word; or emphatic, meaning he quotes in such a way as to emphasize a specific element of a passage. Consequently, the same verse may be quoted multiple times with minor variations. This translation renders Scripture as it appears in the text of Zanchi's Latin treatise rather than quoting from a standard English translation of the Bible.

Another challenge has to do with masculine nouns and pronouns, which Zanchi often used inclusively to refer to both men and women. While he sometimes speaks of "humankind" (*humani generis*) or "people" (*populi*) generically, he more often uses "mankind" or "men" (*homines*) to refer to people of both genders. Whenever possible, this translation has maintained the gendered language in order to stay close to the original text but occasionally the inclusive meaning of a term is emphasized in a footnote.

Additionally, Zanchi understood that the name that God revealed to Moses in Exodus 3:14–19 was properly rendered "Jehovah." He dismissed the common Jewish practice of substituting "Adonai" in place of the divine name and believed that the Hebrew vowel points subsequently added to the text by Jewish copyists provided the correct pronunciation for the tetragrammaton. Nowadays most biblical scholars disagree, seeing "Yahweh" as representing a more likely pronunciation than "Jehovah," but it seems heavy-handed to correct the text in view of Zanchi's strong opinion on the matter.

One final note regarding the translation is in order. In an effort to make this text more accessible to modern readers, it has very occasionally proved necessary to add material in order to clarify meaning or provide background and context. Most editorial insertions in the body of the text have been indicated by placing them within brackets. The exception is that several section headings have been added to the text to improve the visible consistency of the text's structure and aid the reader in tracking Zanchi's argument. All material placed in the footnotes is also editorial, with the following exception: When Zanchi quotes sources in Greek, an English translation has been inserted into the body of the text and the original Greek has been placed in the accompanying footnote.

On a personal note, I have profited over the years from talking about Zanchi with a number of scholars who have contributed—directly or indirectly—to this project, among them John Farthing, Richard Muller, Karin Maag, Paul Fields, Dolf te Velde, Stefan Lindholm, Benjamin Merkle, Christopher Burchill, and Scott Clark. As this project neared completion, I received helpful feedback from Elliot Clark, Jared Mulvihill, Kim Kuhfuss, and Michael Seufert. Richard Bishop kindly helped me navigate some of the patristic sources that Zanchi engages. I am grateful to Jay Collier of Reformation Heritage Books for getting behind this project and to Drew McGinnis, whose labors have made it a better book. My colleagues at Training Leaders International, our students around the world, and those who support our ministry have contributed in ways that defy simple explanation. Suffice it to say, I am honored to spend my workdays in partnership with them.

As I thought about Zanchi's theology of marriage—both physical and spiritual—and as I reflected on his family life, my own wife and children were often on my mind. It has been my greatest earthly joy to share life with them, and I look forward to growing toward maturity in Christ together. I dedicate this little book to Isabel, the littlest one among us, praying that she might remain steadfast in her love for the One who has loved her beyond all measure.

# Abbreviations

ANF      *The Ante-Nicene Fathers: Translations of the Writings of the Fathers Down to A.D. 325*. Edited by Alexander Roberts and James Donaldson. 10 vols. Reprint, Peabody, Mass.: Hendrickson, 1999.

CO      John Calvin. *Ioannis Calvini opera quae supersunt omnia*. Edited by William Baum, Edward Cunitz, and Edward Reuss. 59 vols. Corpus Reformatorum, 2nd series, 29–87. Brunswick: Schwetschke, 1863–1900.

NPNF1      *A Select Library of the Nicene and Post-Nicene Fathers of the Christian Church*. Edited by Philip Schaff. 14 vols. Reprint, Grand Rapids: Eerdmans, 1989–1994.

NPNF2      *A Select Library of the Nicene and Post-Nicene Fathers of the Christian Church*. Edited by Philip Schaff and Henry Wace. 14 vols. 2nd series. Reprint, Grand Rapids: Eerdmans, 1991.

OOT      Girolamo Zanchi. *Omnia opera theologicorum*. 8 tomes in 3 vols. Geneva, 1619.

PRRD      Richard A. Muller. *Post-Reformation Reformed Dogmatics: The Rise and Development of Reformed Orthodoxy, ca. 1520–1725*. 2nd ed. 4 vols. Grand Rapids: Baker Academic, 2003.

# Introduction
## Girolamo Zanchi (1516–1590)
## and *Spiritual Marriage*

During the second half of the sixteenth century, Girolamo Zanchi, a pious and learned pastor, teacher, and theologian, bridged the early and later phases of the movement we call the Protestant Reformation in several critical ways. As the founding generation of Reformers died— Zwingli (1531), Luther (1546), Bucer (1551), Melanchthon (1560), Calvin (1564)—responsibility for leadership fell on the shoulders of successors like Zanchi, who helped guide the Protestant churches of Europe toward maturity. And as the religious landscape shifted rapidly, Protestants found that they needed to develop "a normative and defensible body of doctrine consisting of a confessional foundation and systemic elaboration."[1] If that process sounds dry or obscure, all it means is that, in order to survive, Protestants had to take Reformation insights that had been formulated for pulpits and public debates and recast them for the classroom and in confessional documents.

In order to capture and communicate Reformation ideas in new ways, theologians and educators formulated new pedagogical methods and harnessed old ones to new content. They learned to communicate those ideas at a highly technical academic level so that future ministers could preach the gospel clearly, shepherd Christ's sheep well, and defend the church from error and attack. In practice, this meant the construction of a carefully organized theological system based on Scripture (hence, "orthodox") that could be taught in an orderly fashion in educational contexts like schools and universities (hence, "scholastic"). Along with other late

---

1. *PRRD*, 1:27.

sixteenth-century theologians, such as Zacharias Ursinus (1534–1584), Theodore Beza (1519–1605), and Amandus Polanus (1561–1610), Zanchi played a major role in bridging the gap between the Reformation and the era of Reformed orthodox scholasticism (ca. 1560–ca. 1725).

Zanchi, however, was no talking head or dry-as-dust ivory-tower type. He lived a fascinating life, full of emotional highs and lows, during challenging times. And if, as a scholastic theologian, he tried to talk about God using precise language, he did this out of a deep love for and devotion to Christ and His church. Everyone agreed that Zanchi had a remarkable head for theology. More often than not, however, observers recognized that his theological studies flowed from and into heartfelt piety.

In 1599, for example, when Hendrik Hondius (1573–1650) published a memorial image of Zanchi alongside other luminaries of the Protestant Reformation, Hondius described Zanchi as "second to none in piety."[2] The Puritan Edward Pearse (1633–1673) called him a "learned man" and an "eminent divine," but saw in Zanchi's learning and divinity a finger pointing people toward Christ their heavenly Bridegroom.[3] Pearse's countryman Henry Nelson (fl. 1614) was even more effusive, for he knew Zanchi's academic theology to be "exceeding effectuall" for "all sorts of men." It prevented "curiositie" and speculation and led them "to abandon securitie" outside of Christ. It "rowzed up the drowsie Christian" and helped to "detect the Temporizer; to kindle zeale; to worke vigilancie; to enforce repentance; to minister consolation; to teach the wise; to hearten the weake; to confirme faith and hope of heaven and Happinesse; to daunt ungodlinesse."[4] What a cornucopia of spiritual fruit! And Zanchi's *The Spiritual Marriage between Christ and His Church and Every One of the Faithful* showcases what it looks like for devotional piety and theological precision to be joined in fruitful union.

---

2. Hendrik Hondius, *Icones virorum nostra patrumque memoria illustrium* (The Hague, 1599). See Patrick J. O'Banion, "Jerome Zanchi, the Application of Theology, and the Rise of the English Practical Divinity Tradition," *Renaissance and Reformation*, n.s., 29 (2005): 97–98.

3. Edward Pearse, *The Best Match: or, the Soul's Espousal to Christ* (1673; repr., London: Thomas and Ward, 1839), 8–9, 12, 18, 25, 33, and 64.

4. Girolamo Zanchi, *Speculum Christianum, or, a Christian Survey of the Conscience*, ed. and trans. Henry Nelson (London, 1614), A7v–A8r.

## Life and Times

*Italy*

Girolamo Zanchi was born in the town of Alzano in northern Italy on February 2, 1516.[5] His father was a historian, poet, and lawyer, and his mother was from an ancient family with a good name. He was their only son, and both parents died early—his father when the boy was twelve and his mother three years later—leaving him an orphan. Zanchi had three cousins and an uncle who were part of the religious house of the Augustinian Canons Regular of the Lateran Congregation (not to be confused with Luther's mendicant religious order, the Order of Saint Augustine) located in nearby Bergamo. Everyone agreed that it would be a good place for the boy to learn good morals and good letters. Zanchi, who had enjoyed his studies thus far, was drawn to the house's magnificent library. He soon became a novice and eventually a full member of the congregation.

Around 1536 he went off for additional education, probably to Padua, which boasted a renowned university. Over the next five or so years he studied "Aristotle, languages, and scholastic theology," especially Thomas Aquinas, who became an important influence. By 1541 Zanchi had been ordained a priest and appointed to the office of public preacher for the Lateran congregation, an honor that paved the way for future advancement in the community. In that same year, he was assigned to reside in the Lateran house of San Frediano in Lucca, about two hundred miles south of Bergamo. Sixteen others went with him to Lucca, among them a close friend from Bergamo named Celso Martinengo (1515–1557). They found themselves under the leadership of the house's newly appointed prior, Peter Martyr Vermigli (1499–1562), who was well known for his evangelical ideas and who would soon become a trailblazing Reformed theologian.

Vermigli strongly influenced many of the canons at San Frediano. In 1565 Zanchi remembered how the prior had "publicly commented on the letter to the Romans and privately expounded the Psalms" such that the

---

5. Zanchi's first name is sometimes anglicized as Jerome or latinized as Hieronymus. His last name sometimes appears in its Latin form as well: Zanchius.

members of the community "began to devote [themselves] to the study of the Holy Scriptures, then to the study of the Fathers, especially Augustine" and, finally, "to reading the most learned commentators" of their own day.[6] Zanchi remarked that Vermigli, while he was in Lucca, "loved me and taught me the gospel before any other thing."[7] For Zanchi, Celso, and others the result was that they came to embrace that gospel personally.

Unfortunately, Vermigli's time in Lucca was brief. In 1542, little more than a year after his arrival, the prior and several others fled north into Protestant Europe with the Inquisition on their heels. The reforming work at San Frediano continued but in a diminished capacity and more warily. As Zanchi commented, "For several years we preached the Gospel of Christ in the purest way possible, although [Celso] was guided by the Spirit of God more than me; he always did it more openly and freely."[8] Zanchi also continued his studies and, one way or another, laid his hands on works by Protestant theologians like Philip Melanchthon (1497–1560), Martin Bucer (1491–1551), Wolfgang Musculus (1497–1563), Heinrich Bullinger (1504–1575), and John Calvin (1509–1564). He read the church fathers, mastered Hebrew, and began to study medieval Jewish interpreters of the Old Testament. But by 1549 inquisitorial pressure drove Celso to Geneva, where the town's Italian congregation called him as pastor. Zanchi followed him north two years later and, after an extended Swiss sojourn (during which he met many leading Reformers) and several months of study in Geneva, he landed in Strasbourg as professor of Old Testament and Hebrew at the College of St. Thomas.

*Strasbourg*

Zanchi was staunchly Protestant in his theological sensibilities, but he recoiled at the notion of being attached to one sect or another. "I am not a Zwinglian," he declared, "or a Lutheran or a Calvinist or a Bucerian, but a Christian." And again, "I am neither a Zwinglian nor a Lutheran, since I follow neither Zwingli nor Luther. But I am a Christian, since

---

6. Prefatory letter of Zanchi to Landgrave Philip I of Hesse, October 15, 1565, in *OOT*, 7:4.

7. Girolamo Zanchi to Laelio Zanchi, April 2, 1565, in *OOT*, 8:204–5.

8. Girolamo Zanchi to Laelio Zanchi, April 2, 1565, in *OOT*, 8:204.

I follow Christ."[9] His commitment was to Christ and His church. He read and taught the Scriptures as part of what we would now call the Great Tradition of Christian theology, that is, along with the church universal throughout the ages. Fortunately, his position at the college afforded him the privilege of teaching "freely" (*libenter*), according to his conscience and the Word of God. Unfortunately, under the leadership of Johann Marbach (1521–1581), the city's chief pastor and Zanchi's senior colleague at St. Thomas, Strasbourg was being transformed into a Lutheran stronghold.

A preview of future troubles played out on the day after Zanchi's arrival in Strasbourg. He was invited to dine with several of his new colleagues at the home of Johann Sturm (1507–1589), the rector of St. Thomas. Among the attendees was Marbach, who asserted that praying for the pope is pointless, since he would never convert. Zanchi, however, noted that the only one beyond hope of repentance is he who has blasphemed the Holy Spirit (Matt. 12:31–32; 1 John 5:16). Since none of the attendees at the dinner party knew for certain whether the current pope had committed that sin, they could continue to pray for him. Marbach responded that the pope is the Antichrist, the "man of sin" referred to in 2 Thessalonians 2:3. Zanchi disagreed.[10] This awkward meeting proved the first in a long series of conflicts between the two men.

In the classroom, Zanchi acquired a reputation for moving through the biblical text at a glacially slow pace. His method was rigorous and expansive, in part because he sought to integrate doctrinal and exegetical theology with biblical theology, polemics, and apologetics. He was tasked with lecturing on the Old Testament beginning with the Latter Prophets, but after nearly a decade in the classroom he had covered only the first twelve chapters of Isaiah and all of Hosea, along with some psalms and part of 1 John. Yet, he was no sluggard. In addition to his regular teaching

---

9. *Miscellaneorum liber primus*, in OOT, 7:262, 265. In his inaugural lecture at Strasbourg, Zanchi made a similar point (*OOT*, 8:221).

10. Joseph N. Tylenda, "Girolamo Zanchi and John Calvin: A Study in Discipleship as Seen through Their Correspondence," *Calvin Theological Journal* 10 (1975): 105–7; and Charles Schmidt, "Girolamo Zanchi," *Theologische Studien und Kritiken* 32 (1859): 630–31.

obligations, he lectured on Aristotle's *Physics*, presided over more than twenty public disputations, and was frequently called upon to cover his colleagues' courses.

Other demands occupied Zanchi's attention outside of the classroom. In late 1553 he was called to serve as an elder for the city's refugee congregation, and he preached regularly to the small group of Italian attendees. As part of this work, he spearheaded efforts to raise money to care for refugees and also threw himself into efforts to promote unity within the visible church. No less significantly, Zanchi married. His bride was Violanthis Curione, the daughter of an old friend from his days in Lucca. Sadly for Zanchi, who was deeply committed to marriage both theologically and personally, domestic life entered a long rough patch. The couple suffered a first miscarriage in May 1554 after barely seven months together. A second miscarriage followed in March 1555, which caused partial paralysis in Violanthis's body. She never fully recovered. He wrote to Heinrich Bullinger in Zurich, "My wife miscarried and sickened almost unto death, and my heart was greatly disturbed as were my studies, but the Lord was merciful—not only to her but also to me (for now she is beginning to improve)."[11] Various expensive remedies were attempted, putting the household in an embarrassing financial state. Yet, in November 1556, after three years of marriage, Violanthis died. Some months later, Zanchi received word that his old friend Celso had died as well.

We might consider it shocking that Zanchi remarried quickly, probably within a year of Violanthis's death, but this was not unusual for his context. His second wife was Livia Lumaga of Piuro in the Rhaetian Freestate north of Italy. The groom claimed in a letter to Calvin that he could have had a German wife from a noble family with a large dowry, but out of love for his "own nation" he instead chose a poor Italian to wed.[12] By November 1558 she had given birth to twin sons, both of whom died within three months. Zanchi wrote to Wolfgang Musculus

---

11. Christopher J. Burchill, "Girolamo Zanchi in Strasburg 1553–1563" (PhD diss., Cambridge University, 1980), 50.

12. Zanchi to Calvin, March 30, 1559, in CO, 17:484.

of his own grief but especially of his wife's: "She is a woman; she is young; she is a new mother; she is in a foreign country." Unable to understand the language, she could not even receive the consolations offered by those around her.[13] A daughter was born in 1559, but she died three years later. In due course, children came and survived to adulthood, but the couple's first years were heavy with grief.

These marriages and deaths played out for Zanchi alongside a frustrating series of conflicts with Marbach. During Zanchi's time at St. Thomas in Strasbourg, Lutheran theologians came to a consensus on a variety of theological issues, among them the doctrine of the real presence of Christ in the Lord's Supper. Beginning in the 1550s some Lutherans began formulating a doctrine of ubiquity to explain Jesus's words at the Last Supper, "this is My body" and "this is My blood" (Matt. 26:26, 28). In other words, when asked the question, What happens to the bread and wine? these Gnesio-Lutherans (as they became known) responded that they truly remained bread and wine. But they went on to argue that in addition to bread and wine, communicants also received Christ's physical body in, with, and under the elements. How? His human nature appropriated the divine attribute of immensity so that it was physically present everywhere, albeit in a special way in the Lord's Supper.

Gnesio-Lutherans formulated their position against Roman Catholics on the one hand (who believed that the bread and wine were miraculously transformed into the body and blood of Christ) but also against Reformed theologians like Zwingli (who regarded the bread and wine as signs pointing to Christ) and even Calvin (who argued that believers received Christ's body spiritually in the Supper by faith but that He was not physically present in the bread and wine). For Gnesio-Lutherans, it was ubiquity or nothing. In Strasbourg this position was particularly controversial since the town's first generation of Reformers—men such as Martin Bucer and Peter Martyr Vermigli— had embraced neither ubiquity nor the Gnesio-Lutheran understanding of the Supper that followed from it.

---

13. See Zanchi to Wolfgang Musculus, November 1558, in *OOT*, 8:146.

Not surprisingly, then, Marbach had good reason to suspect that Zanchi, with his strong ties to Zwingli's Zurich, Calvin's Geneva, and Vermigli himself, would balk at the doctrine of ubiquity. To nip that problem in the bud, in 1554 Marbach demanded that Zanchi subscribe to the Lutheran Augsburg Confession (1530). The Italian was reluctant to do so because he believed that, if he signed, he would no longer be able to teach freely, according to his conscience and the Word of God. After several months of delay, he finally consented but with the proviso that he bound himself to the confession only, as he stated in his subscription, insofar as it was "understood in an orthodox manner."[14] Marbach regarded this as the equivalent of Zanchi signing with his fingers crossed.

By January 1561 Marbach had lodged formal complaints against his colleague, claiming that Zanchi erred in his teaching on the sacraments, election, the perseverance of the saints, and eschatology. Marbach directly questioned Zanchi's integrity, orthodoxy, and salvation. He labeled him a Zwinglian and Calvinist but also (and more offensively) a Schwenckfeldian, Anabaptist, and Novatian. According to one sympathetic observer, despite all that he had to endure, Zanchi "persevered strongly, bravely, and vigorously in the work of the Lord."[15] The complex controversy that ensued consumed more than two years of Zanchi's life. In the end, he was exonerated, as theologians from around Protestant Europe rallied to support him. Even the Lutheran professors at Tübingen refused to accuse him of heresy. But despite winning the debate in the wider court of theological opinion, Zanchi lost within the local contexts of Strasbourg's city church and the College of St. Thomas.

*Rhaetia*

Over the years, Zanchi had been offered pulpits and lecterns at Geneva, Bern, Lausanne, Zurich, Lyons, Marburg, and Heidelberg but had refused them all, believing that his "primary responsibility lay with the church in Strasbourg."[16] Now, to the relief of many, a new opportunity presented

---

14. Zanchi to Calvin, July 1563, in *OOT*, 8:153.

15. François Hotman to Heinrich Bullinger, January 11, 1558, in *CO*, 16:384.

16. Burchill, "Zanchi in Strasbourg," 189.

itself. Zanchi was offered the pastorate of the Reformed congregation of Chiavenna in the Rhaetian Freestate, near his wife's hometown. The Strasbourg Senate granted him permission to leave. With some reluctance and many regrets for what might have been, he accepted the call and departed in November 1563. His opponents celebrated their victory. The theological fault lines that separated Marbach and Zanchi in Strasbourg eventually hardened into the divide that still separates Lutheran and Reformed churches.

For Zanchi, being a pastor in Chiavenna turned out to be just as frustrating as being a professor in Strasbourg. His congregation included not only the local Reformed community but also a wide variety of exiles from Italy seeking refuge. These included both orthodox Protestants and "all kinds of enthusiastic spirits, humanistic freethinkers, and rationalists."[17] To make matters worse, Zanchi also had to deal with an incumbent assistant pastor who believed that his time served should have entailed seniority over the new man. The next few years saw Zanchi (and his congregation) weather division, plague, and heresy. He was frustrated to discover various streams of anti-Trinitarian theology filtering into the region along with some of the Italian refugees. "It's not difficult to see," he lamented, "whence comes the evil and who promotes it—Spain produces the hens and Italy hatches the eggs; we can already hear the chicks peeping."[18]

The troubles came to a head in 1567 when a large contingent in his congregation, stirred up by the assistant pastor, colluded to exclude all foreigners from election to church office. Zanchi called it an "open schism" and protested that qualified candidates could not be denied simply on the basis of where they had been born.[19] He refused to back down and, although Zurich, Geneva, and a local synod endorsed his position,

---

17. Lukas Vischer, "Girolamo Zanchi, reformierter Prediger in Chiavenna," *Bündnerische Monatsblätter* 10 (1951): 290.

18. Zanchi to Bullinger, August 19, 1565, in *Bullingers Korrespondenz mit den Graubündern*, ed. Traugott Schiess (Basel: Basler Buch und Antiquariatshandlung, 1905), 2:627. The reference to Spain was, presumably, meant to indict Miguel Servetus (d. 1553), who rejected classical Trinitarian theology.

19. Vischer, "Reformierter Prediger," 297.

he lost his pulpit. Deeply disappointed and hurt, he wrote to Bullinger, "I have never experienced anything more unfair."[20] Bullinger agreed, lamenting to a friend that Rhaetia "didn't have many Zanchis" and could hardly afford to lose this one.[21]

Yet, Zanchi landed on his feet and in September 1567 accepted an offer from Elector Frederick III of the Palatinate (r. 1559–1576) to teach at the University of Heidelberg. By February of the following year, he and Livia were ensconced in their new home and his inaugural lecture had been delivered. He needed a doctorate to occupy the chair in theology, so in June Frederick granted him one. Zanchi joked to Ludwig Lavater of Zurich that, previously, he had been a theologian without a ring or a license or a cap but that now he was a lord doctor—ringed, capped, and licensed.[22]

*Heidelberg*

These were fruitful and pleasant years for Zanchi. His job was to teach theology "from holy scripture and the church fathers, by means of common places," which proved to be a good fit for his talents and interests. His colleagues, students, and patron appreciated his work.[23] Zanchi thrived among them and was appointed rector for 1571. He and Livia also filled their home with children. In July 1576, at age sixty-one and nearly ten years after arriving in Heidelberg, he wrote to an old acquaintance from his Strasbourg days that he was "still alive," and "by the blessing of God in good health for [his] age." He heartily thanked God for the gift of "a wife and five children, besides one who, I hope, will shortly make its appearance." He requested prayer that God would "both replenish [Zanchi's family] with the gifts of His Spirit and supply

---

20. Zanchi to Bullinger, June 23, 1567, in *Bullingers Korrespondenz*, 3:14.

21. Bullinger to Tobias Egli, July 4, 1567, in *Bullingers Korrespondenz*, 3:15. As for the assistant pastor, he "soon proved intolerable" to the fickle Chiavennese congregation and was dismissed. Vischer, "Reformierter Prediger," 300.

22. Zanchi to Lavater, June 22, 1568, in *OOT*, 8:185.

23. Luca Baschera and Christian Moser, introduction to *De religione christiana fides – Confession of Christian Religion*, by Girolamo Zanchi, ed. Baschera and Moser (Leiden: Brill, 2007), 1:10.

them with what is needful for their passing honorably through this present life."[24]

During these years not only was Zanchi teaching and raising a family, he was also finding that he had a gift for writing. In the summer of 1570 Frederick III was startled to discover that anti-Trinitarianism was spreading in his lands, and he commissioned Zanchi to write a defense of the orthodox doctrine of the Trinity. With astonishing speed (given his pace in the lecture hall), Zanchi composed and published a massive treatise in two volumes entitled *On the Three Elohim, or, on the Eternal Father, Son, and Holy Spirit, One and the Same Jehovah*.[25] Rather than a straightforward defense of the Trinity responding to contemporary debates, Zanchi's book was a positive, elaborate, and exegetically based formulation of the doctrine that signaled "a return to the theological tradition, to the fathers and to the medieval theologians—and even to the classical philosophers—in the interest of establishing a correct use of the terminology of trinitarian doctrine in the exposition of its scriptural foundations."[26] The book was a success. And if Reformed Protestantism's commitment to classical orthodox Trinitarianism now seems natural, this is in no small part thanks to Zanchi.

He had always been a careful and deep thinker, but something of a plodder, often unoriginal in his conclusions and hesitant to put anything in print.[27] While at Strasbourg, he had explained his failure to publish:

> There seemed to me almost more writers these days than readers. Nor could I fail to notice the deplorable situation that our city has more teachers than students, the forests have more hunters than beasts, and the courts have more lawyers than clients. There was another reason [for not publishing]: my disposition is such that I

---

24. Zanchi to Edmund Grindal, July 22, 1576, in Hastings Robinson, ed., *The Zurich Letters*, 2nd series (Cambridge: Cambridge University Press, 1845), 498.

25. *De tribus Elohim, sive de uno vero Deo aeterno, Patre, Filio et Spiritu Sancto, uno eodemque Iehova* (Frankfurt, 1572).

26. *PRRD*, 4:84–85.

27. On Zanchi's failure to publish during the Strasbourg years, see Christopher J. Burchill, "Girolamo Zanchi: Portrait of a Reformed Theologian and His Work," *Sixteenth Century Journal* 15 (1984): 191–92.

prefer to read the writings of others to publishing my own works for others to read, especially since I observed that our age has so many carping critics that not even the most careful and definitive works are safe from their nitpicking. Thirdly, so many learned and wise men are publishing scholarly and polished works that I was not only ashamed to put forward my own writings, but I also saw that my writings were probably unnecessary and of little value to today's Church. I put off publication for the day when it could profit the Church more than now. Finally I would never have thought that the doctrine which I have taught and defended from the beginning would sometime come to be questioned and condemned by anybody here, otherwise I would have published it and submitted it to the judgement of the churches.[28]

But now Zanchi found he had something to say, and over the remainder of his life he became remarkably productive. His collected works contain some 6,000 folio columns of small and tightly packed type—biblical commentaries, polemical works, a confession of faith, treatises on discrete theological topics, addresses and lectures, and several volumes of a massive but sadly incomplete Reformed *Summa* of theology—most of it written in the last eighteen years of his life and all of it published after his fifty-fifth birthday.

*Neustadt*

Zanchi's sojourn in Heidelberg eventually came to an end as well. Most sixteenth-century Europeans assumed secular magistrates were responsible for supporting true religion and suppressing false ones. Thus, when Frederick III's son and successor as Elector Palatine, Ludwig VI (r. 1576–1589), declared himself a Lutheran, it spelled trouble for Zanchi and his colleagues. Following Frederick's death in 1576, the university's Reformed professors were purged for "teaching Calvinism up to this point."[29]

---

28. Zanchi to the Strasbourg Scholarchs, n.d. [1563], in *OOT*, 8:157. I quote from John Patrick Donnelly's translation in his "A Sixteenth Century Case of Publish or Perish/Parish," *Sixteenth Century Journal* 6 (1975): 112–13.

29. Kenneth Austin, *From Judaism to Calvinism: The Life and Writings of Immanuel Tremellius (c. 1510–1580)* (Aldershot, U.K.: Ashgate, 2007), 170.

Fortunately, Frederick's second son, Johann Casimir (1543–1592), favored the Reformed and established a new school, known as the Casimirianum, in a former Augustinian monastery on the other side of the Rhine River at Neustadt an der Hardt. The honor of giving the inaugural lecture in May 1578 fell to Zanchi, who also occupied the chair of New Testament. In the classroom, he began a series of lectures on the Pauline Epistles that took him through Ephesians, Philippians, Colossians, and 1 Thessalonians.

When Elector Ludwig died in 1584, his son and successor Frederick IV (1574–1610) was too young to rule, so the reins fell into the hands of his uncle, Johann Casimir, Zanchi's lord and patron. Invited to return to his duties at Heidelberg, the old Italian found the offer less appealing than it might once have been, for he had begun to show his age. Zanchi described himself as "a decrepit old man but nevertheless in good health by God's grace."[30] In fact, his eyesight was failing and he suffered from other ailments as well, all of which slowed his scholarly work and must have made teaching laborious.[31] Having traveled enough for one lifetime, he chose retirement and remained behind in Neustadt, living at a property he purchased with proceeds from *On the Three Elohim.*[32]

In 1590, now completely blind and relying entirely on the aid of an amanuensis to continue writing and editing, Zanchi sent one last treatise to the printers for publication, *The Spiritual Marriage between Christ and His Church and Every One of the Faithful.*[33] He had written several works focused on Christology during the final years of his life, and *Spiritual Marriage* was part of that effort. It had its origins, we assume, in his Neustadt lectures on Ephesians 5:25–30, but at heart it was a defense against the Lutheran doctrine of ubiquity. In the months before his death, Zanchi revised the material and, in August, penned a dedicatory letter to

---

30. Zanchi, *De religione christiana fides—Confession of the Christian Religion*, ed. Luca Baschera and Christian Moser (Leiden: Brill, 2007), 1:92.

31. See his comments in *De spirituali inter Christum et ecclesiam, singulosque fideles connubio* (Herborn, 1591), iir–v.

32. Burchill, "Portrait," 204–5n106.

33. *De spirituali inter Christum et ecclesiam, singulosque fideles connubio* (Herborn, 1591).

Horatio Palavicino (ca. 1540–1600), a wealthy Genoese merchant living in Elizabethan England.

That fall, with the manuscript of *Spiritual Marriage* off his desk, Girolamo Zanchi made a final trip to visit friends in Heidelberg. He was seventy-four years old, completely blind, limited in mobility, and in failing health. He died peacefully on November 19, 1590, and his body was interred in Heidelberg's university church. Those who raised his epitaph knew him well enough to prioritize his heart's deep affection above the massive tomes he had written:

> Here lies buried Hieronymus Zanchius,
> > exiled from Italy, his fatherland, for the love of Christ.
> How great a theologian and philosopher he has been,
> > is witnessed by his many books,
> > by those whom he taught in the schools,
> > and by those who heard him instruct the churches.
> And now, although his spirit has departed,
> > yet he has remained with us by his illustrious name.[34]

After a lifetime in exile, his soul found its true home, at last, in his Savior.

### *Spiritual Marriage*

*Spiritual Marriage* seems to have begun its literary life as a theological excursus in Zanchi's massive commentary on the book of Ephesians. But that commentary was only published years after Zanchi's death, when his sons and heirs worked through his notes and laboriously published almost everything he had ever composed—whether previously published or not—in an eight-volume *opera omnia*. As we saw, Zanchi sent the stand-alone manuscript of *Spiritual Marriage* to the printer in 1590. We do not know why he chose to extract this specific material from his lecture notes on Ephesians. Nor do we know how substantially he revised the material he had originally delivered to his students.

---

34. This translation is by Otto Gründler, "Thomism and Calvinism in the Theology of Girolamo Zanchi (1516–1590)" (ThD diss., Princeton Theological Seminary, 1961), 15.

Shortly after its initial publication in 1591, just months after Zanchi's death, *Spiritual Marriage* was translated into English and published in Cambridge by the university's printer. Two years later it appeared in French from Geneva.[35] In the sixteenth century, the rapid translation and republication of a theological treatise from Latin into multiple vernacular languages signaled its potential value and appeal to a broad audience—not just scholars and ministers but laypeople too. Those who came after Zanchi also found his reflections on spiritual marriage valuable, and we can hear echoes (and sometimes find actual citations) of his work in later publications on similar themes. So, what was it about this particular treatise that appealed to publishers, translators, readers, and writers? And why bother to make it available in modern English translation after more than four centuries?

### The Heavenly Bridegroom and His Bride

The short answer to both questions is its lively depiction of a spiritual reality: that Christ is the church's one and only Bridegroom and that the church collectively—that is, every person who has true and living faith in Christ individually—is Christ's bride. What is more, although *Spiritual Marriage* draws readers into highly complex theological debates, it is neither abstract nor speculative. Instead, Zanchi took a pastoral approach, emphasizing the significance—both immediate *and* eternal—of the subject matter for Christians. Like the apostle Paul, he labored to beget Christ in his readers again and again (Gal. 4:19; 1 Cor. 4:15). By reminding them of what was true—that Christ always loves and cares for His bride, that no better Husband could exist—he endeavored to "nourish the growth of believers in faith and love, and thus to deepen the intimacy and assurance of their union with Christ."[36]

---

35. It was also, of course, included in the various Latin printings of the Ephesians commentary (1594, 1601, 1888–89), which was incorporated into volume 6 of the various editions of Zanchi's *OOT* (1605, 1613, 1617–19, 1649).

36. John Farthing, "*De coniugio spirituali*: Jerome Zanchi on Eph. 5:22–33," *Sixteenth Century Journal* 24 (1993): 651. J. V. Fesko has also explored Zanchi's theology of spiritual union in "Jerome Zanchi on Union with Christ and Justification," *Puritan Reformed Journal* 2 (2010): 55–78; Fesko, *Beyond Calvin: Union with Christ and Justification in Early*

Describing the relationship between Christ and his church as a marriage may feel somewhat unusual to us. Surely, we think, we wouldn't want to push *that* metaphor too far! We may be more comfortable with categories like justification, sanctification, and glorification. Zanchi liked those terms too; he deployed them as part of his understanding of the Christian faith, integrated them into his theological system, and distinguished them from union with Christ. But he was often drawn to talk about spiritual marriage, probably because it provided a rich source of biblical vocabulary with which to describe what it meant to be a Christian. In this, he was no innovator.

Over the centuries, Christian writers have found the marriage metaphor to be a rich source for meditating on God's love for His people and the nature of the relationship into which He has drawn them in His Son. And exegetes have long recognized the heavenly Bridegroom as a major theme in Scripture that is useful for the church's encouragement and comfort. Bernard of Clairvaux (1090–1153), for example, made much of it in his sermons on the Song of Songs, where he saw the passionate union of lover and beloved as symbolic of the equally passionate love between Christ and the church.[37] Calvin made hearty use of the theme of spiritual marriage in his Ephesians commentary and elsewhere.[38] Other writers and preachers found the marriage theme prevalent in Psalm 45; Hosea 2; Matthew 25:1–13; Mark 2:18–22; Luke 5:33–35; John 3:22–36; 1 Corinthians 6:12–20; 2 Corinthians 11:2; Ephesians 5:22–33; and Revelation 21–22, among other passages. Whatever our level of comfort, following the lead of Scripture, the church has long recognized the suitability of marital language for talking about our relationship with Christ, for meditating on its significance, and for framing our prayer.

---

*Modern Reformed Theology (1517–1700)* (Göttingen: Vandenhoeck & Ruprecht, 2012), 207–26; and Fesko, "Girolamo Zanchi on Union with Christ and the Final Judgment," *Perichoresis* 18 (2020): 41–56.

37. See, for example, Bernard's "Sermons on the Song of Songs 83," in *The Essential Writings of Christian Mysticism*, ed. Bernard McGinn (New York: Modern Library, 2006), 257–61.

38. See Farthing, "*De coniugio*," 646–47; cf. Dennis E. Tamburello, *Union with Christ: John Calvin and the Mysticism of St. Bernard* (Louisville: Westminster John Knox, 1994), 84–101.

*Love and Marriage*

Some readers may be uncomfortable using marital language to describe our union with Christ because even the best earthly marriages are very imperfect. Husbands can domineer or withdraw. Wives can subvert or manipulate. Both parties retreat emotionally and physically. We know too many stories of loveless marriages that stay intact "for the sake of the children" only to collapse when the nest is emptied, just as we also know couples who lose their passion for one another and seek fulfillment elsewhere, regardless of the children. In an age of easy divorces, starter marriages, and shacking up, it is sometimes difficult to see the point of matrimony. All we need is love, or so we're told. And if we have it, we tell ourselves, we have enough. But what if that satisfyingly warm feeling of contentment and connection with the one lying next to us diminishes? Should we not be true to ourselves and get on with finding it somewhere else? Many enter into marriage with the assumption—either tacit or explicit—that they will remain united only so long as they feel themselves to be "in love."

That feeling of being in love, which too often passes for the reality, is a fleeting thing. It is a far cry from how Scripture envisions love and is not what we should expect from our own marriages. The problem is not merely that we have too low a view of marriage but also that we set the bar of our expectations for marriage too high. We place too heavy of a burden upon the union by expecting our spouse to satisfy the deepest longings of our heart. Once we realize our spouse cannot—first, because that's not his or her job and, second, because our hearts were not designed to find ultimate fulfillment in any creature—our eyes begin to wander; we look elsewhere for satisfaction. The biblical mandate that calls a husband to love his wife as his own body, giving himself up for his bride as Christ loved the church (Eph. 5:25–28), and that calls a wife to submit to her husband as to Christ (5:22), offers a rather different perspective.

For Paul in Ephesians 5, and for Zanchi, our earthly marriages are like a mirror. They fulfill their truest purpose by drawing our attention toward the real thing: the spiritual marriage between Christ and His church. In other words, our earthly marriages only make sense when our union with Christ remains in view. We begin to understand something of that higher and heavenly union by paying attention to the biblical witness—to the Genesis account of Adam's marriage to Eve, to pertinent Old Testament laws, and to the teachings of Jesus and His apostles. These make us aware that the temporary earthly unions we encounter here below reflect a heavenly pattern. They point away from themselves. The delicious irony is that, ultimately, we can only understand and fully enjoy our earthly marriages when we view them in light of our spiritual union with Christ.

That truth was something that Zanchi knew experientially as well as theologically. We might wonder, for example, how he found it within himself to care for an incapacitated wife who required constant attention for nearly their entire marriage. Why did he virtually bankrupt himself, spending his savings and Violanthis's dowry on doctors, medicines, and treatments to alleviate her suffering? How could he (and his wives) endure miscarriages, stillbirths, and the deaths of their young children? He could do it because he was looking to and trusting in his heavenly Bridegroom and not his earthly brides. Zanchi did not expect Violanthis or Livia to satisfy him at the deepest levels of his heart. This reality opened the way for a rich domestic life filled with enduring love and joy.

We should not imagine that Zanchi's home was idyllic, but he genuinely enjoyed marriage and fatherhood, and he remained committed to his family through thick and thin. He sought the prayers of his spiritual friends on his family's behalf and lamented the loss of those who predeceased him. Thirty years into his second marriage, he still doted on his "venerable Livia," lauding her as "the most loving mother of all our children" and, to him, "my most dear wife in the Lord."[39] He spoke in "glowing terms" of the privileges and benefits of life together and viewed procreation as only one of the many "comforts and blessings" that accompanied marriage.[40] After Zanchi's death, his sons and sons-in-law (with, one must imagine, the encouragement of his daughters) spent nearly three decades transforming their father's notes into a coherent and publishable collection of theological treatises and a monument to his memory for the

---

39. Zanchi, *De religione*, 1:100.
40. Farthing, "*De coniugio*," 651.

benefit of the church. The prodigious amount of time, money, and energy invested in that project signals their devotion to him even more clearly than their words in the dedicatory letters of those volumes.

*Men and Women*

In addition to Zanchi's use of marital language to describe the relationship between Christ and the church, another reason why we might be tempted to disregard what he has to say is that some of it feels dated. Many modern readers—even those who embrace what we now call traditional gender roles—may chafe at some aspects of how Zanchi characterizes the relationship between husbands and wives. For example, he speaks of the husband as the wife's "lord and savior"—not language that we regularly appropriate for earthly marriages. Likewise, although Zanchi recoils at the notion of a woman being forced into matrimony against her will, he assumes that marriages are primarily contracted between the bride's parents and her prospective groom. He anticipates that her consent proceeds primarily out of her deference to the will of others. In short, he often casts women merely as supporting actors; they seem to exist mostly in relationship to their husbands or fathers.

If, on that account, the book feels dated, that is because it is four hundred years old. Zanchi and his *Spiritual Marriage* need no defense for having been shaped by their own times and cultural context. But we should, nevertheless, be willing to listen carefully to what Zanchi says, for so much of it is fresh and invigorating. As C. S. Lewis reminds us, reading old books is like having "the clean sea breezes of the centuries blowing through our mind," and we often are better able to recognize the errors of our own age having been given a dose of something from a previous one.[41]

Moreover, it is worth noting that if Zanchi characterized the relationship between husband and wife as one that involved both headship and submission, he did so—following Paul in Ephesians 5:23—because Christ is the head of the church, which is His body. Zanchi's purpose was to recall the close connection between our marriages here below and the heavenly and eternal one between Christ and His church. Because

---

41. C. S. Lewis, introduction to *On the Incarnation: The Treatise* De Incarnatione Verbi Dei, by Athanasius (Crestwood, N.Y.: St Vladimir's Seminary Press, 1996), 5.

Christ is the church's Lord and Savior, Zanchi was willing to apply those same terms to earthly husbands with respect to their wives. This interpretive move allowed him to highlight the spiritual significance of earthly marriage and set it apart as a special institution established by God that matters here and now because it points both men *and* women to the gospel. For, when it came to the individual believer's union with Christ, Zanchi was clear that gender was not an issue. Women were just as truly and immediately united to Christ by faith and by the Spirit as were men.

Note, too, that Zanchi believed earthly marriage was meant to be a happy estate for both parties. It was not good for either of them to be alone. In marriage everything that belonged to one spouse became the joint property of the other—both in prosperity and adversity. He wrote, "There are various crosses and troubles" to be endured, among them "poverty, death, exile, cares, injuries—suffered both at the hands of those close to home as well as at the hands of strangers." Zanchi's household experienced its fair share of these crosses and knew they were better faced together than alone. Of course, they also knew "many consolations and blessings," and these were the sweeter for being enjoyed together.[42]

*Exegesis and Interpretation*

A final challenge that faces readers of *Spiritual Marriage* is Zanchi's exegetical method. Early modern Reformed exegetes agreed that Scripture was to be read according to its "literal sense," but discerning that literal sense did not mean for them (as it may for us) simply reading the text "according to the constraints of grammar, history, literary method."[43] Recognizing that Scripture had both human and divine authors, they did not think it possible to properly interpret it merely by determining what the human author meant. Thus, they understood the literal sense to be "constructed" or "compounded." That is, the biblical texts have both a "simple literal sense" that "consists of the immediate grammatical, historical and literary meaning of the very words of Scripture"

---

42. Zanchi, *De connubio*, 39–40.

43. Herman J. Selderhuis, "Introduction to the Psalms," in *Psalms 1–72*, ed. Herman J. Selderhuis, vol. 7 of *Reformation Commentary on Scripture*, ed. Timothy George and Scott M. Manetsch, Old Testament (Downers Grove, Ill.: IVP Academic, 2015), xlvi.

and a "spiritual sense" consisting of the "meaning of the very words of Scripture in light of the full form and content of Scripture." These were inseparable but distinguishable, and the simple served the spiritual.[44]

Various rules restrained how expositors like Zanchi read and interpreted the Bible. The so-called rule of faith—the "trinitarian, christological, and evangelical scope of Scripture's content and the meaning that arises from it and in turn makes sense of the whole and the parts" was one important principle.[45] But following a ruled interpretation of the Bible did not mean that everyone read each text in exactly the same way. In fact, a spectrum of interpretative approaches existed among Reformed readers of Scripture. Calvin, for example, focused on grammatical and historical considerations before moving on to christological readings when the text provided warrant for doing so, and he dismissed "some of the more imaginative ruled readings as 'too forced.'"[46] But other orthodox Reformed theologians interpreted the Bible in a more straightforwardly Trinitarian, christological, and evangelical way.

Although Zanchi respected Geneva's Reformer immensely and looked to him as a mentor, his approach differed from Calvin's.[47] Knowing ahead of time that all of the Scriptures were about Jesus (Luke 24:27), when Zanchi read the Bible, he expected to find Christian theology, and Christ Himself, in the text of both the Old and New Testaments. Sometimes this commitment led him to discern scriptural allegories, shadows, and mysteries that pointed to Christ but that would not have been apparent to Calvin. In this, Zanchi was also influenced by the more allegorical traditions of medieval exegesis, which he imbibed as a canon of the Lateran Congregation and while studying theology at university. Calvin, having been formed more as a Renaissance humanist than a medieval theologian, had neither of those experiences.

---

44. Selderhuis, "Introduction," xvii. See also David C. Steinmetz, "The Superiority of Pre-Critical Exegesis," *Theology Today* 37 (1980): 27–38.

45. Craig S. Farmer, "Introduction to John 1–12," in *John 1–12*, ed. Craig S. Farmer, vol. 4 of *Reformation Commentary on Scripture*, ed. Timothy George and Scott M. Manetsch, New Testament (Downers Grove, Ill.: IVP Academic, 2014), li.

46. Selderhuis, "Introduction," li.

47. See Tylenda, "Girolamo Zanchi and John Calvin," 101–41.

This means that we may be surprised by some of Zanchi's interpretations. According to him, Adam's rib signified Christ's deity, and the flesh that filled the empty cavity when it was removed signified His humanity. Similarly, Zanchi follows a long tradition of interpreters who concluded that Eve was not made from the bones of Adam's feet (lest she be trampled underfoot) nor from his skull (lest she exercise dominion over him) but rather from his rib, specifically so that he would love her from his heart. While this interpretation is delightful in its fancy, few modern readers find warrant for it in the text.

Interpretations like these might cause us to raise our eyebrows and wonder whether or not we can trust Zanchi as a faithful expositor. As his readers, however, we should reflect on three important points that will help us get the most out of what he has to say. First, Zanchi read the Bible as part of a long tradition of interpretation stretching back to the church fathers and coming, by way of medieval theologians (of whom he was both critical and appreciative), into the sixteenth century. He was even up to speed on Jewish interpretation of the Old Testament. In other words, if we decide that he went wrong in his readings, at least he wasn't just making things up as he went along. Second, Zanchi was more hermeneutically self-aware than many of his contemporaries. Part of the reason why he plodded along so slowly in the lecture hall was because he followed a carefully mapped-out course for interpreting biblical texts.[48] We need not delve into the details of that method here; the point is simply that he had one. His method grounded his biblical exegesis and restrained truly fanciful interpretations. Third, and finally, just because Zanchi's interpretation of a text strikes us as unusual or differs from the way we have learned to read Scripture, we should not assume that we are right and he is wrong. It may be that the history of interpretation took a wrong turn somewhere during the last four centuries and that an old Italian exile approaching the end of his days still has a thing or two to teach us.

---

48. Zanchi described his approach to interpreting Scripture, which drew upon the methodological work of the logician Jacopo Zabarella (1533–1589), in his 1568 inaugural lecture at the University of Heidelberg (*OOT*, 8:212–19).

# The Spiritual Marriage between Christ and His Church and Every One of the Faithful

# Dedicatory Epistle

To the most noble man Horatio Palavicino,[1] gilded knight,
Girolamo Zanchi prays for grace and peace.

As the proverb says, most noble and generous Horatio, "Better late than never." And, "Soon enough done, if well enough done." Therefore, I will not have been entirely and absolutely worthy of criticism for withholding until now this public congratulations, which I owed to you long ago to congratulate you after your successful undertaking before both of our most illustrious princes, for that office with which your most serene queen adorned you, that you might truly be Her Majesty's gilded knight. For, although I desired it, it was not possible more quickly either for my secretary to transcribe this book or for it to be brought to light by the printer. Add also the many troubles of mind and the considerable number of inconveniences that have befallen and frequently do befall me in my old age and that slow my honest study and pious endeavors a great deal. In fact, from experience I daily learn and perceive that statement to be most true: "Fear old age, for it does not come alone."[2]

---

1. Palavicino (ca. 1540–1600) was a Genoese merchant and aristocrat who moved to England during the reign of Mary Tudor (r. 1553–1558). He became immensely wealthy and served Elizabeth I (r. 1558–1603) as an ambassador, spy, investor, and royal financier both in England and on the Continent. He was knighted by Elizabeth in 1587. See Ian W. Archer, "Palavicino, Sir Horatio (c. 1540–1600)," in *Oxford Dictionary of National Biography,* online ed. (Oxford University Press, 2004), https://doi .org/10.1093/ref:odnb/21153.

2. φοβοῦ τὸ γῆρας, οὐ γὰρ ἔρχεται μόνον.

What good man and knight will, therefore, blame an old man just because he walks less quickly than a youth? So what if old age is united with blindness, weakness of the legs, and other diseases too? Among the planets, to be sure, Saturn never complains that it completes its course more slowly than the others, since it is moved according to its own natural order and position. Therefore, my congratulations, although late, nevertheless ought neither to be blamed by anyone nor to go unappreciated by you. Should not this, which, as you see, was accomplished by a slow-paced and feeble old man (albeit one not yet entirely destitute of all the warmth of natural inclination), be all the more agreeable and delightful for being the later and, therefore, the less expected by you? For I consider not only the office itself—as it is in itself and how great it is—but also, and this first of all, I weigh who bestowed it upon you and for what reasons. And for all of this I consider that congratulations must be given to you, and I heartily congratulate you.

To be the gilded knight of some prince or other is, certainly, a great office. Moreover, to be the knight of a queen is greater. But by far the greatest is to be of such a queen who is neither the least nor the smallest jewel of the Christian world. The queen is Elizabeth, born of kings into a kingly court, and trained in royal customs and the pure and true religion, in great erudition of letters, in the knowledge of languages, and, finally, adorned with royal and heroic virtues: with the greatest piety, incredible clemency, invincible courage, and abundant generosity to pious men. In a word, she is a queen most dear to the Lord Jesus Christ. What more could you want?

Christ made obvious and manifest to the whole Christian world His love for her by many and great benefits (pertaining to both the soul and the body as well as to external things), all of them gathered together in her, such that I need not list or exhibit them, especially to you, who knows all these things better than me. Certainly, on its own a steadfast profession and defense of true Christian piety, and a manner of life in accordance with it, should satisfy us and each of the pious. For this divine gift of true piety is a sure testimony of Christ's eternal and constant benevolence toward us. Nevertheless, I beseech you meanwhile to consider that the Lord Jesus Christ snatched her, that is, Elizabeth, from the jaws of the lioness,[3] saved the one He snatched, and made a queen of the one He saved. Through this one whom He made queen, He restored to Himself His pure teaching and true worship, ruled the people happily, and preserved them in the greatest peace for many years—about thirty-two at present. He exposed and averted innumerable crafty snares of the devil against her and her kingdom; scattered the most atrocious machinations and wicked councils of her foes; shattered the greatest strengths of her enemies and routed them; also defended neighboring people; and fostered, sustained, saved, and continues to sustain and save pious princes. How great is that testimony?

Moses was beloved by God and chosen for the redemption and the great preservation of God's people. Therefore, when all the male infants of the Hebrews in Egypt were destroyed, on account of the tyrannical command of the king—and that for no other reason than because they were Hebrews and in order that, at last, the whole people of God might finally be extinguished—Moses's life was preserved by the marvelous providence of God through the midwives themselves, who were otherwise foreigners to the people of God.[4] He was rescued from the waters. He was adopted as a son by the daughter of the king. He was educated in the royal court as the king's progeny. He was adorned and protected by heroic and truly divine virtues, power, wisdom, fortitude of soul, and other innumerable gifts. He was established as the liberator and leader of the people. He preferred to suffer with the people of God than to live in royal finery with the wicked [Heb. 11:25]. He, therefore, saves the people.

---

3. Presumably, Zanchi refers to Mary Tudor, Elizabeth's half sister, a zealous persecutor of Protestants, and queen of England from 1553 to 1558. As heir apparent to the throne and a suspected Protestant, Elizabeth represented both a political and religious threat to her sister's regime. Consequently, Mary kept Elizabeth under close watch and often under house arrest.

4. Zanchi follows a Jewish tradition that understands the midwives in Exodus 1:15–21 to have been Egyptians not Hebrews. The tradition runs through the Septuagint (ταῖς μαίαις τῶν Εβραίων; Ex. 1:15), Josephus (*Antiquities*, 2.205), the Vulgate (*obstitreces Haebrorum*), and various rabbinic interpreters and is argued on the basis of variant vocalizations. See Moshe Lavee and Shana Strauch-Schick, "The 'Egyptian' Midwives," *TheTorah.com*, December 27, 2015, https://thetorah.com/article/the -egyptian-midwives. I am indebted to my colleague Dr. Paul Smith for clarifying this otherwise obscure point.

He withstands the tyrant. He drowns him in the Red Sea with his whole army. He destroys the enemies. He receives the law from God. He delivers the heavenly teaching to the people. He renews His true worship. He removes idolatries. He cleanses everything. He revives the true invocation of God. Finally, he leads the people in committing themselves to the right way of submitting and of obtaining the inheritance promised to the patriarchs.

These things God did through Moses. But has He not clearly declared to all how great was His love toward Moses and all of His people? Indeed, concerning those things that were done and handed down in the Old Testament, the apostle says, "Whatever things were written, were written for our instruction, in order that through patience and the consolation of the Scriptures, we might have hope" [Rom. 15:4]. Certainly, nowadays, when I behold—having others guide my eyes—your queen, I consider that something not dissimilar has happened and is happening. And I understand clearly that such a one might be God's handmaiden, or rather the bride of Christ, through whom He supplied, and today still supplies, so many great things to His church.

Is it not enough then, O most distinguished man, to have made yourself such a servant of such a queen? With those things supplied to you by the wisest and most prudent queen, I now join[5] this congratulations, so as not to have supplied it to you rashly. For she saw that the dignity of your nobility, of your strength, of your faithfulness and diligence in executing her affairs was justly deserving, lest the dignity with which you shine be any less than that which adorns you, that you might not be less worthy of it than it is of you. For that best of queens did not by this honor ennoble you from ignobility. Rather she ennobled you from nobility, and while she wanted to bestow a new dignity upon you, she repaid your merits. And likewise, our friendship demanded that I congratulate you for all this. Do you see, then, most prudent Horatio, that my congratulations, although late, nevertheless cannot and ought not deservedly be unpleasant to you? And for that reason, it should be

_______________

5. *coniungo.* This word plays an important role in Zanchi's subsequent discussion of spiritual marriage.

most acceptable to you, for hardly do I send it to you naked but rather clothed and, indeed, covered with a noble garment.

For I send with it a certain treatise of mine concerning the spiritual marriage between Christ and the church and every one of the faithful. It is contained in a certain small book, but is, nevertheless, most honorable and most noble on its own and by itself.

But I wish this dedicated to your name chiefly for a twofold purpose. First, that some perpetual testimony might exist in the church of my regard for you and, in turn, that my soul might be encouraged by remembrance of your regard for me and for my books, especially for the one that, accepted into your trust and care, you have taken with you to the most honorable and most noble kingdom of England. Second, that amid such and so many controversies at this time concerning the Christian religion, you might have a summary from me of our salvation with which you might be able to defend and protect yourself against all enemies.

For our entire salvation consists in this spiritual and divine marriage. For Christ the Bridegroom always delights in His bride. He is her Head and everlasting Savior, that she might not utterly fall away from Him. He says by the prophet, "I will betroth you to Me forever" [Hos. 2:20]. And, says Christ, "I prayed for you, Peter, ἵνα μὴ ἐκλίπῃ your faith" [that your faith may not fail; Luke 22:32]. Indeed, with faith that never utterly fails, who will be lost? Just so, by this steadfast faith, true union with Christ is so contracted, fostered, and safeguarded that it will never be destroyed. It will be most gratifying to me to have known that my congratulatory gift has, indeed, been gratefully received by you, that the Graces might not be wholly naked.[6]

For, indeed, the world does not lack those who love the inscriptions of good books and procure thanks that thereby they might see something added to the fame and glory of the splendor of their names. But, to say the least, they who care excessively for such things reveal by words and deeds that they do not care for themselves. But, most excellent Horatio,

---

6. ἵνα μὴ παντάπασιν αἱ Χάριτες γυμναί. Zanchi here combines an allusion to the Luke 22:32 reference above (ἵνα μὴ) with the ancient Greek proverb "the Graces are naked," which is roughly the equivalent of "Don't look a gift horse in the mouth."

it is less your true and ancient nobility and ancestral virtue than your individual piety and your devotion to obtaining eternal salvation through Christ that causes me to think and hope something rather different of you. So, read and reread.

Farewell, and continue to love me, as you do, and to have my son Titus Cornelius commended to you, which is a mark of your steadfastness in loving and doing good.

Neustadt. The first of August, in the year of Christ 1590, but the seventy-fifth year and sixth month of the author.

# Introduction

Whatever is conveyed in various passages of Holy Scripture concerning the church's origin and her spiritual marriage with the Son of God, the apostle deduces, explains, and confirms from the first creation of humankind, as from a fountain of the mysteries of Christ, when, in the epistle to the Ephesians, chapter 5, he says, "Husbands, love your wives even as Christ loved the church" [v. 25], and so forth.[1] For Moses recounts

---

1. This first section of the treatise orients the reader to Zanchi's theological method. Zanchi defined "theology" as "the doctrine of God taken from the Word of God." That definition emphasizes the role of Scripture, which, in turn he defined as the "foundation of the whole of theology, upon which the whole body of Christian doctrine is established [*fundatum*] and built up [*extructum*]; indeed, the whole is gathered and joined together out of the Scriptures." Zanchi, *De sacra Scriptura tractatus integer*, in *OOT*, 8:319. Proper theological method for Zanchi is, therefore, twofold: analytic (or "resolutive") and synthetic ("compositive"), and Zanchi employs both methodological approaches throughout his commentary on Ephesians. As Benjamin Merkle explains, Zanchi applied this twofold method to Scripture via "an initial analytical stage of 'resolution' in which a close reading of the biblical text moves from exegesis of the passage to the creation of a list of questions or propositions addressed by the author of the text. This resulted in a *locus communis* for the particular passage, and represented the 'resolution' of the text. The next step, the 'composition' stage, involves the elucidation of a particular *locus*, moving from that general principle back to an assortment of biblical passages for 'confirmation and illustration' of the proposition. The result of Zanchi's approach is a method that hovers between, and draws from, both the synthetic elements of scholastic theology and simple textual exegesis." Benjamin Merkle, *Defending the Trinity in the Reformed Palatinate: The Elohistae* (Oxford: Oxford University Press, 2015), 83. See also Dolf te Velde, *The Doctrine of God in Reformed Orthodoxy, Karl Barth, and the Utrecht School* (Leiden: Brill, 2013), 85–88; *PRRD*, 1:181–89; 2:499–510; and Otto Gründler, "Thomism and Calvinism in the Theology of Girolamo Zanchi (1516–1590)" (ThD diss., Princeton Theological Seminary, 1961), 27–36.

the story of how Eve was created from Adam while he slept and, later, was given to him in matrimony. He recounts how, when Adam saw her, he said, "This is now bone of my bone and flesh of my flesh" [Gen. 2:23]. And, finally, he recounts a general principle about the marriage of humans—both among themselves and with the Son of God—which is in operation until the end of the world and is pronounced with these words: "For this shall a man leave his father and his mother, and shall cleave to his wife, and they shall be two in one flesh" [v. 24].[2] The apostle understands these words in such a way that he interprets them as referring to Christ and His church when he says, "This is a great mystery, but I am speaking about Christ and the church" [Eph. 5:32]. For we are flesh of Christ's flesh, and bones of His bones, just as Adam said of Eve.

So, in order to speak of the spiritual and heavenly marriage between Christ and the church and each one of the faithful, I must first examine that passage from Moses about Eve's creation and the first institution of carnal marriage and diligently consider how each and every particular may correspond to spiritual things.[3] For both the creation of Eve (drawn from the rib of Adam while he slept) and the carnal marriage contracted between Adam and Eve were manifest types both of the spiritual creation of the church (which was drawn from the side of Christ while He was dead on the cross) and also of the contracting of the marriage between Christ and the church. Next, the whole doctrine of human marriage needs to be divided briefly and plainly into chapters so that thereby all

---

2. In Zanchi's reading of Genesis 2, he sees the author (Moses) narrating Adam's progress through a learning experience that reflects the analytic approach described in the previous note. Moses moves from a description of the event of Eve's creation, to Adam seeing and identifying her as "bone of my bone and flesh of my flesh," and, finally, to Adam drawing a "general principle" about marriage based on his experience and his analysis of that experience. But, says Zanchi, whereas Adam (as described by Moses) proceeded analytically in Genesis 2, in Ephesians 5, Paul proceeded synthetically by deducing, explaining, and confirming what Scripture taught concerning the origins of the church and her spiritual marriage to Christ.

3. When Zanchi uses the word "carnal" in this treatise, he is merely describing earthly marriages in contrast to the spiritual marriage of Christ and His church. "Carnal," then, does not have a negative connotation here, for although Zanchi understands earthly marriages to be temporary shadows of things to come, he nevertheless held them in high esteem as God's good gift and as a mystery pointing to the believer's union with Christ.

may understand more easily what they should discern with regard to the divine marriage between Christ and His church. And, finally, the doctrine of the spiritual marriage must be explained and confirmed, having been examined according to the heads of doctrine of carnal marriage.[4]

And I will set forth all of these in certain brief theses, whereby readers will be able to more easily understand and remember them.

---

4. Here Zanchi indicates his plan to proceed both analytically (resolutively) and synthetically (compositively) in this treatise, moving from an examination of a specific text (Gen. 2:24) to develop a *locus* about carnal marriage and then to consider that *locus's* relationship to related *loci*—in particular spiritual marriage—in order to explain it, following Paul in Ephesians 5:25. Finally, he intends to return to Scripture to illustrate and confirm the findings of his synthetic work.

# Chapter One

# The Creation of Eve and Her Marriage to Adam

The substance of the history of Eve's creation and of the matrimony contracted between her and Adam, and how those things which Moses wrote concerning the first marriage may correspond with the spiritual one, upon which the apostle expands

With regard to the first point that pertains, the following must be regarded as the foundation that the apostle hands down in Romans 5[:12–21] and 1 Corinthians 15[:45–49], namely, that in this marital matter, the first Adam and the second Adam (that is, Christ) must not be considered as private individuals but rather as two first principles.[1] From the one proceeded and proceeds all of humankind. From the other was and is born the church. And that first man was the type and figure of the other, that is, of Christ. Wherefore, we should consider those things that Adam did prior to sin not so much ἱστορικῶς [in the manner of history] as μυστικῶς [in the manner of a mystery].[2] Therefore, I divide into three parts the history of Eve created from Adam while he slept and then brought to Adam once awake that he might take her in matrimony.

---

1. *duo prima principia.* The parallel between Adam and Christ was already an important motif among Reformed theologians, and later writers within the tradition further explored the biblical theme of representative headship to develop a sophisticated system of covenant (or federal) theology.

2. Zanchi argues that, on the basis of Romans 5 and 1 Corinthians 15, we have warrant to interpret Genesis 2 as pointing to something beyond the mere historical facts of Eve's creation and marriage to Adam. For more on the use of the so-called *sensus mysticus* (mystical sense) among the Reformed orthodox scholastic theologians and its relationship to the *sensus literalis* (literal sense), see *PRRD*, 3:477–82.

The first of these concerns the counsel of God—why He did not want Adam to be alone; why He created Eve from Adam, specifically from his rib; and, finally, why He gave Eve to Adam in marriage.

The second concerns the creation of Eve herself and the manner of her creation.

The third concerns the leading of Eve to Adam and their marriage.

## The Counsel of God

Concerning the first part, Moses wrote thus: "And Jehovah Elohim said, 'It is not good that man should be alone. Let Us therefore make a helper for him, that may be before him'" [Gen. 2:18], which is to say, "like him in all things and always ready to submit to him."

Theses:

1. The reason, then, why God would not have Adam to be alone was because this was not good.

2. It was not good, that is, it was not in itself becoming or proper, that he who was to be the head of all humankind should live among all the living creatures and in the world as a man on his own.

3. Neither was it good, that is, delightful for Adam himself, to pass a solitary life in this wide world.

4. Neither was it good, that is, profitable either for Adam himself or for all of his posterity, which God surely could have created without the works of man and woman—but then what love and affinity of souls would there have been among mankind?

5. Finally, it was not good because it was the counsel of God that from the seed of the first man Adam, a second Adam, Jesus Christ, should be conceived and born.

Therefore, with good reason God made Adam a helper who was like him and who would always be subject to him and especially ready for all honest duty and submission.

6. But why did God not create Eve in some other way than out of Adam himself, even of his rib? The reason is expressed by the apostle in Acts 17[:26], namely, that all men might (by propagation) be of one origin, as members of one head, and thus that all humankind might be as

one body and of the same nature.[3] The apostle says, "He made from the one man all humankind to dwell on the whole face of the earth."

7. Again, He formed her of Adam's rib so that, in addition to other reasons, Adam might love her more, being his own flesh, which is what Adam himself pronounced when he said, "This is now bone of my bones, and flesh of my flesh" [Gen. 2:23]. From here, the apostle derives his argument for loving our wives, namely, because they are our flesh [Eph. 5:28].

8. The wife should not exercise dominion over the husband; therefore, she is not taken from the head. Neither should she be trampled underfoot; therefore, she is not created from the feet. But rather she should be loved from the heart, and, therefore, she was taken from the rib, which is near the heart.[4]

9. Notwithstanding, Moses adds to this the reason why He gave her in matrimony to Adam: so that she might be a helper unto him [Gen. 2:18].

10. A helper, I say, first for the living of an honest, pious, and pleasant life.

11. A helper also for begetting children and multiplying mankind on the earth.

---

3. Zanchi may have had pre-Adamite thinkers in his sights here. Late sixteenth-century thinkers who endorsed this view alleged that only certain peoples on earth were descended from Adam. This led some adherents to conclude that non-Adamic peoples—typically, native inhabitants of the Americas and sub-Saharan Africans—were not created in God's image or that they did not bear His image to the same extent as Adam's descendants. Zanchi's point that all were of "one origin…and of the same nature" argues against the superiority of any group. As Bishop Richard Kidder noted in 1694, the single origin of all humankind was meant to ensure that "men might not boast and vaunt of their extraction and [origin]…and that they might think themselves under an obligation to love and assist each other as proceeding from the same original and common parent." Richard Kidder, *A Commentary on the Five Books of Moses* (London, 1694), 1:6. See Philip C. Almond, *Adam and Eve in Seventeenth-Century Thought* (Cambridge: Cambridge University Press, 1999), 49–60.

4. Cf. Thomas Aquinas, *Summa Theologica*, 1.92.3. The Swiss Reformer Johannes Oecolampadius also incorporated this reading of the significance of God using Adam's rib to form Eve in his *In Genesim enarratio* (Basel, 1536), 39r–v, and it remained popular into the seventeenth century. See Almond, *Adam and Eve*, 148.

12. A helper, finally, for fulfilling the decree of God with regard to the creation of His church and with regard to Christ, the head of the church, thence begetting and, hence, establishing, propagating, and enlarging the kingdom of God.

Thus far the first section, which explains the counsel of God—why He did not want Adam to be alone, why He decreed to create Eve from Adam, and, finally, why He resolved to give her to him in marriage.

If you accommodate what we have said regarding God's plan and apply it to Christ and His church, this counsel of God will appear yet more splendid.

13. It was not good that the first Adam should be alone. Much less ought the second Adam to be alone, for He was made man in order to be the new head of the new elect body unto eternal life and to be the first-born among many brothers [Rom. 8:29], so that just as through one man sin entered into the world and death through sin, so by this second man might righteousness and life everlasting overflow to many [Rom. 5:12].

Therefore, in order that the head should not be alone without members, He needed to have the body of the church, like Him—not only in human nature but also in holiness, having neither spot nor wrinkle—and subject to Him, and also a helper, bearing heirs of the heavenly kingdom even to the end of the world.

14. God willed to create Eve from Adam himself, and make her flesh of his flesh, and bone of his bones [Gen. 2:23], and, by her help, thence to bring forth all humankind, first for this cause, that all mankind might be from one head and source.[5]

15. So also Christ wanted, from His own side—and when John explained this mystery (as it were), he said that blood and water flowed from Christ's side, which truly is the substance of the church's salvation and regeneration [John 19:34]—from His side, I say, Christ wanted the church to be created spiritually, and thus to be made flesh of His flesh and bone of His bones, so that those who would become the heirs of the heavenly kingdom, even the whole church, might all be of one head.

---

5. *principio.*

16. Again, God wanted Eve to be created from Adam, so that Adam might be more disposed toward her in love.

17. So Christ wanted the church to be created from His side so that He might be more and more disposed toward loving us, just as His own flesh.

18. The first reason why is expressed in Hebrews 2[:11]: For He who sanctifies (that is, Christ) and they who are sanctified (that is, the church) all have one source.

For just as Christ, no less than other men, is of the one Adam with regard to the nature of His flesh, so we are of the one Christ—flesh of His flesh and bone of His bones—with regard to spiritual regeneration.

19. And so we are flesh of His flesh and bone of His bones, that by Him we might possess every heavenly blessing, even to such an extent that no one can boast of possessing any heavenly blessings except that he possess them by way of Christ, directed unto him by way of Christ Himself as from a head.

20. The second reason is assigned by the apostle in Ephesians 5[:29]: No one ever hated his own flesh, but nourishes and cherishes it, even as Christ does the church because we are flesh of His flesh and bone of His bones.

21. Lastly, the particular reason why God brought Eve to Adam and gave her to him as wife was so that by her help, as if by his own work, he might beget sons and so fill up the earth with men.

22. Thus, God the Father gathered the church and gave her to Christ, that by her ministry He might daily beget new sons unto Himself, wherewith the kingdom of heaven might, at length, be filled.

Thus, with regard to the first part of the history set down in Genesis 2, we see the counsel of God wherein He would not have Adam to be alone but instead gave him a helper, taken from none other than Adam himself. How very well this counsel corresponds with His counsel concerning Christ. For He did not want Christ, having been made man, to be alone, but rather wanted to give the church to Him as spouse, begotten from none other than Christ Himself, even from His own flesh and blood through the Holy Spirit. So it was appropriate that there should be two heads—one of humankind according to the flesh; the second of the people of God according to the Spirit. Thus far the first part.

## The Creation of Eve

The second part of that history in Genesis 2 contains the creation of Eve herself from Adam's rib. Thus, this is set down: Moses says that when, from among all living creatures, Adam could not find any that could be a true helper to him and who could stand in his presence, "Jehovah God, therefore, caused a heavy sleep to fall upon the man, and he slept, and He took one of his ribs, and closed up its place with flesh, and Jehovah God made the rib that He took from the man into a woman" [vv. 21–22].

This is the substance of it:

Theses:

1. Eve, whom God willed to be Adam's wife, was created of none other than Adam himself.

2. This is the manner of her creation: God caused Adam to fall into a deep sleep, and, while he was sleeping, God drew out one of his ribs, filled in the empty place with flesh, and formed the woman from the rib.

3. A short while ago, the reason was given why Eve was made from Adam's rib—namely, because God did not want the source[6] from which humankind would proceed to be diverse in kinds. Therefore, He wanted Eve also to be derived from the one Adam, that all men might be from the one man.

4. In this respect, Adam was a true type of Christ, for just as Eve and all humankind were from Adam, so from Christ, as from one single source, the whole church always was and is begotten. And this is what the apostle says, interpreting Christ's words, "We are flesh of Christ's flesh and bone of His bones" [Eph. 5:30].[7]

---

6. *principium.*

7. Many modern scholars conclude that the portion of Ephesians 5:30 quoted here was not part of Paul's original letter but rather a later scribal interpolation. John Muddiman argues for the dissenting view: "A large number of MSS (including ℵc D P G, as well as Irenaeus, the old Latin and the Syriac Peshitta) add after 'his body' **part of his flesh and bone.** (The phrase in Greek is literally 'out of his flesh and bone')…. It is not difficult to see why the words, if originally present in the text, would be omitted: that

Therefore, the bride has nothing except what she receives from Christ, her Bridegroom and Head, and she is a partaker in His nature [2 Peter 1:4].

5. But why did He will to create Eve from Adam in this particular way? Certainly, God could just as well have removed a rib from Adam and formed Eve from it while he was awake. But He did not want to do so on account of the mystery of things to come, concerning which the apostle says, "This is a great mystery" [Eph. 5:32].

6. For the slumber, the deep sleep sent by God upon Adam, was a type of Christ's death.[8] For if the sleep of David described in Psalm 3[:5] was a type of Christ's death—which is how Augustine and, after him, Luther and others explained that passage, as concerning the death and resurrection of Christ—how much more was the first Adam's slumber a type of the second Adam's death.[9]

---

Christians are the Body of Christ is standard doctrine; but the extension 'part of his flesh and bone' would seem very strange to a later scribe who had failed to pick up the allusion to Gen. 2.23, where Adam says of Eve, 'This at last is bone of my bone and flesh of my flesh.' Accidental omission is also a possibility." He concludes that "the shorter text" is "probably secondary." John Muddiman, *A Commentary on the Epistle to the Ephesians* (London: Continuum, 2001), 286 (emphasis in original). Whether the phrase is original to the letter or not, as Zanchi perceives, Paul certainly had Genesis 2 in view.

8. A similar interpretation of Adam's slumber being significant on account of its typological relation to Christ's death was offered by Peter Martyr Vermigli, *In primum librum Mosis* (Zurich, 1569), 12r. Subsequently, this interpretation was embraced by, among others, George Walker, *God Made Visible in His Works, or, a Treatise of the External Works of God* (London, 1641), 197–98.

9. "It is not inappropriate to notice that the use of the 'I' expresses the idea that Jesus underwent death of his own volition in accordance with his statement, *For this the Father loves me: because I lay down my life that I may take it up again. No one takes it away from me; I have the power to lay it down, and I have the power to take it up again* (Jn. 10:17–18). What Christ said was this: you did not arrest me and put me to death as though against my will; no, *I rested and fell asleep, and I arose because the Lord will uphold me.* The scriptures contain countless examples of 'sleep' being used to mean 'death.'" Augustine, *Expositions of the Psalms*, trans. Maria Boulding, ed. John E. Rotelle (Hyde Park, N.Y.: New City, 2000), 1:78–79 (emphasis in the original) (cf. *NPNF1*, 8:5). Similarly, Luther indicated that he "will interpret [Psalm 3] concerning Christ, being moved so to do by the same argument that moved Augustine—that the fifth verse does not seem appropriate to apply to any other than Christ." *Standard Edition of Luther's Works* (Minneapolis: Lutherans in All Lands, 1903), 1:105–6.

7. For sleep is the image of death, wherefore in the Holy Scriptures the dead are said to be sleeping.

8. Therefore, just as the material whence Eve was formed was taken from the sleeping Adam, so also from Christ, dead on the cross, blood and water flowed, whereby the church is washed from her sins, conceived, and born again, made flesh of Christ's flesh and bone of His bones. Her birth is by blood; her washing is by water.

9. But when we say that the church is derived and created from the side of the dead Christ, this has a double meaning. First, we may understand it in terms of merit, because it was at that point that Christ by His blood merited and obtained from the Father the remission of sins and rebirth unto eternal life for all the elect—all who ever were or shall be, of whom alone the church consists.

10. Second, in terms of imparting, which is in baptism.

11. For baptism is a sacrament of rebirth, and the material[10] of our rebirth is the blood of Christ, dead on the cross, for us.

12. Thus, the apostle says in Romans 6[:3]: "Do you not know that as many of us as are baptized into Christ Jesus are baptized into His death?"

13. Therefore, because the power of Christ's death and blood (whereby we put off the old man and put on the new and are made new creatures) is communicated to us in true baptism, which is by water and Spirit, for that reason, when we are reborn in baptism, each of us is at that time said to have become bone of Christ's bones and flesh of Christ's flesh.

Now, behold the mystery of Eve taken out of and created from Adam's rib when a deep slumber overtook him and he slept.

14. To this pertains what Isaiah says, "When His (the Messiah's) soul makes an offering for guilt, He shall see a long-lived seed" [53:10].[11] For

---

10. *materia.* Zanchi uses the Aristotelian term *materia* to refer to the material that makes a thing what it is.

11. Zanchi quotes Isaiah 53:10 from the Vulgate (*Si posuerit pro peccato animam suam, videbit semen longaevum*) rather than from the *Testamenti Veteris Biblia Sacra* (London, 1581) of Immanuel Tremellius and Franciscus Junius (*quandoquidem exponebat seipse sacrificium pro reatu; dicens, videbit semen, prolongabit dies*).

all of the elect are reborn from Christ's death and blood, and thus will it be until the end of the world. This is the meaning of "long-lived seed."

15. This accords with what Christ Himself said, "Unless the grain of wheat falling into the ground dies, it remains alone. But if it dies, it brings forth much fruit" [John 12:24].

This "much fruit" is the church, which has the same nature as a dead grain of wheat, and which is made flesh of Christ's flesh by participation in His death and blood.

16. There is another mystery: Eve was made from Adam's rib, which was a hard bone, but the empty place was filled with flesh.

17. The rib—and this is how the godly fathers understand it—signified the strength of Christ's deity; the flesh signified the weakness of His human nature. As Peter says, Christ communicates His divine nature to us [2 Peter 1:4] and strengthens us. He, however, takes upon Himself our weaknesses.

18. Therefore, Christ's divine nature is signified by the bone, but His humanity is signified by the flesh. Thus, the apostle refers to both, saying, "bone of bones, flesh of flesh" [Eph. 5:30], because in regeneration we become partakers of His divine nature [2 Peter 1:4] and so too is our flesh (that is, our nature) renewed and sanctified; it becomes a changed flesh, that is, it becomes Christ's flesh.

19. Also, the reference to "building" that Moses makes when he says, "And Jehovah God built that rib into a woman" [Gen. 2:22] has a mystery of its own, for it signifies the building of His vast temple, which is the church. Concerning this, Ephesians 2[:22] says, "In which you also are built together into the dwelling place of God." And also, 1 Corinthians 3[:9]: "You are God's building."

20. The foundation of this building is that most powerful of rocks, Christ, whose strength and fortitude was, as I said, signified by the rib.

Thus far the second part of the history from Genesis 2, in which Eve's creation is described and the regeneration of the church adumbrated as well.

## The Union of Adam and Eve
The third part follows, in which the union itself is described.

This part includes, first, the betrothal of Eve to Adam specifically, for Moses says, "And He led her (Eve) to Adam himself," namely, so that he might take her in marriage [Gen. 2:22].

There is an emphasis here—*to Adam himself*—as if to say, "to him from whom she was taken." Therefore, God betrothed Eve specifically to Adam so that she might, for a second time, more and more, be made one flesh with him from whose bones she was made bone of his bone.[12]

Second, this part includes Adam's consent to this union and the celebration of the union. Adam knew her as his wife and his flesh. Moses expresses this, saying, "And Adam said, 'This now is bone of my bones'"— that is, This bone and this flesh is my flesh and bone and also of my flesh and bones—"'Therefore, she will be called אשה, *'ishah* [woman], because she was taken out of man'" [v. 23].

Third, it includes the institution of matrimony granted to all humankind and teaches how exclusive the marriage bond is. For thus Adam proclaims, saying, "For this reason, one shall leave his father and mother…and they will be (two) in one flesh," that is, they will be one flesh [v. 24]. But, as interpreted by the apostle, this is understood to refer principally to Christ and the church.

Fourth, it includes the quality of the first estate wherein Adam and Eve existed before the fall. He says, "They were both naked, and they were not ashamed" [v. 25].

All these things contain the mystery of the marriage that would exist between Christ and the church.

*The Betrothal of Eve to Adam*
1. The Father betroths the church to none but Him from whose side she was also taken and, through regeneration, made flesh of His flesh and bone of His bones, that is, to Christ.

2. For it was improper for her to grow together more and more into one flesh with anyone other than Him from whose flesh and bones she was made, by regeneration, His flesh and bone.

---

12. For a discussion of Zanchi's contemporaries describing God as the divine matchmaker between Adam and Eve, see Almond, *Adam and Eve*, 155.

3. Therefore, in this marriage it should be noted: who betroths, whom He betroths, and to whom He betroths.

4. It is God who betroths, for He brought Eve to Adam. John 6[:44]: "No one comes to Me unless the Father draws him." And for this He uses only the ministry of men called to it, such as the apostles and other ministers of the gospel: "I betrothed you to one husband, to present you a chaste virgin to Christ" (2 Cor. 11[:2]).

5. But whom does He betroth? He betroths only those whom He previously chose in Christ, those He redeems by Christ's blood, those He regenerates by the Holy Spirit, those He buries and makes alive with Christ in baptism. For it was to Adam that He brought Eve, who was created from Adam's own rib (and none other's).

6. Therefore, only those who have been born again by Christ's blood and made flesh of Christ's flesh can truly be called Christ's bride.

7. And to whom does He betroth? To Christ alone. Therefore, He alone is the church's Bridegroom. Here is the reason: because from His side alone flowed the blood and water whereby we are cleansed of our sins and, being born again, made new creatures—flesh of His flesh and bone from His bones. For this reason, Moses says, "And He (God) led her (Eve, now created) to Adam himself," to him, indeed, of whose rib she had been formed [Gen. 2:22].

8. And how does He betroth? By giving faith, whereby we know Christ, embrace Him, and subject ourselves to Him. "I will betroth you to Me in faith" (Hos. 2[:20]).[13] For the consent of the bride is also

---

13. Again, Zanchi follows the Vulgate, which translates the Hebrew הָנוּמֶאֶבּ ("in faithfulness") as *in fide* ("in faith"). Note that, in his commentary on Hosea, Immanuel Tremellius translated the Hebrew as *cum fide* ("with faith"), however, he was aware that the Hebrew word he translated as *fide* "is taken from firmness [*firmitate*], whence others interpret it: 'I will betroth you to me in firmness.'" Tremellius, *In Hoseam prophetam interpretatio et enarratio* (Lyon, 1563), 40, 67–68. The *Biblia Sacra* of Tremellius and Junius renders the phrase "and I will betroth you to me [by?] faith," leaving the preposition indeterminate but governed by the ablative form of *fide*. Zanchi's own commentary on Hosea glosses "in faith" as follows: "But I will betroth you to me by way of faith [*per fidem*] and you will know the Lord," explaining that the word *fidem* indicates "true and firm [faith], by which we truly assent to the judgment of the law concerning sins and to the gospel concerning grace and to the free remission of sins by way of Christ [*per Christum*] and by which we call upon the well-disposed God." Later, he notes that the Hebrew

required in this. Wherefore, when Moses says, "He led her," we should understand that she was not reluctant but consenting. And the verb וַיְבִאֶהָ, *vayebi'eha*, communicates this—"He caused her to come."

9. But God betroths us to Christ not because He is persuaded by any of our merits but merely out of His goodness and mercy. Therefore, it says, "I will betroth you to Me in mercy and compassion" (Hos. 2[:19]).

10. Also, both His creation of Eve from Adam's rib and, once she was created, His betrothal of her to that same Adam—both of these proceed from His goodness and grace.

11. Nevertheless, as I said, He requires our consent. Yet this He also gives, having given us faith. For He works in us to will [Phil. 2:13]. All these things are to be gathered from those words, "And He led her to Adam himself" [Gen. 2:22].

And this is the first of the mysteries contained in the third part of this pregnant history.

*Adam's Consent and the Celebration*

In the second place, it also contains Adam's consent and, in that consent, the celebration and perfection of the marriage. For Adam says, "This is now also my bone and flesh" (on account of the marriage) "and of my bone and from my flesh" (on account of the creation from his rib).

12. Adam, therefore, knew Eve as his wife. For when he saw that God willed this, and when he also saw Eve's consent and willingness, he willed it as well. And out of the concursus of these three wills—God's, Eve's, and Adam's—the marriage was contracted. So, he declared, "This now is bone of my bones."

13. But this is truly and perfectly fulfilled in Christ and the church. God's eternal will comes first, for God leads us to Christ. He stirs up the will within us, so that we might consent to this spiritual marriage. And Christ the Bridegroom can will nothing but that which His Father also wills [John 5:30; 6:38]. Thus, He accepts us as His bride, and He knows us as His flesh and bones, saying, "This is bone of My bones."

---

word is understood to refer to "constancy and firmness [*firmitudine*] in matrimonial faith [*fide matrimoniali*]." Zanchi, *In Hoseam commentarium* (Neustadt, 1600), 58, 202 (*OOT*, 5:17, 56).

14. Herein pertains John 6[:37]: "All that the Father gives to Me will come to Me, and whoever comes to Me I will not cast out."

First, He says, "All that the Father gives to Me"—the will of the Father. Second, He says, "those that the Father gives will come to Me"—the will of the elect, of the bride. Third, He says, "those that come to Me I will not cast out"—the will of Christ the Bridegroom. With these three wills the spiritual union between us and Christ is achieved.

15. Wherefore, as Adam knew Eve as his bride and flesh, saying, "This now is bone of my bones," so Christ knows us as His bride and flesh, and He loves, cherishes, and nurtures us as such. For the apostle, by the Spirit of Christ, says plainly, "We are flesh from His flesh and bone from His bones" [Eph. 5:30].

16. Thus, when Paul was persecuting His bride, the church of the faithful, Christ said to him, "Saul, Saul, why are you persecuting Me?" [Acts 9:4]. As if to say, "In persecuting the church, you are persecuting Me, My flesh and My bones."

17. And it should also be noted that when Adam said, "This is now bone…," he intended to indicate that the most exclusive of all unions existed between him and Eve, for Eve was both his flesh on account of the union and flesh of his flesh on account of her generation from him.

18. What could be more exclusive than this double binding? For a person can be your flesh but not be of your flesh, such as your wife, who was someone else's daughter and born of another's blood. Moreover, a person can be of your flesh but not be your flesh in the same way as your wife, such as your son or daughter. But for one person to be both your flesh (as a man and his wife) and of your flesh (as children are), this is, of all bonds the most exclusive.

19. And such a bond there never was—save Eve with Adam alone and the church with Christ alone.

20. So, when the apostle assigns the very words of Adam to Christ with reference to His church, he means to indicate that between Christ and us is the greatest and most exclusive of unions, for we are both Christ's flesh (by way of marriage) and flesh of His flesh (by way of regeneration).

21. But what is the purpose of this? That faith, hope, and love might increase in us. Faith—our love for Christ, the flesh of whose flesh we

are. Hope—for eternal life, because where the husband is, there is the wife; where the head is, there is the body as well. Love—for since we are all flesh of Christ's flesh, we ought to love Him and ourselves, and to embrace one another in sincere love.

22. But based on this passage, it also appears that a certain distinction should be made between regeneration and betrothal because regeneration precedes betrothal, at least according to the order of nature. For first Eve was made from Adam's rib and then, afterward, she was given to him in marriage.

23. Certainly, one can be regenerated without the preceding consent of his own will. But no one can be married to Christ and embrace Him as husband without faith and without his own consent, for the consent of both parties is essential in marriage. But we cannot consent unless our will is renewed, unless good is made from evil and willingness from our unwillingness.

*The Institution of Matrimony and Its Exclusivity*

In the third place, the last part of this mystical history[14] contains the institution of marriage and what the man must do in order to be joined to his wife: "For this reason," it says, "a man must leave his father and mother and cleave to his wife, and they shall be (two) in one flesh" [Gen. 2:24].

24. The apostle interprets this chiefly as referring to Christ and the church, and he says that it is a great mystery [Eph. 5:32].

25. For it was on this account—that is, so that He might be one flesh with us and us with Him through spiritual marriage—that Christ first left God the Father. How? Paul explains in Philippians 2: "Being in the very form of God…He emptied Himself, taking the form of a servant" [vv. 6–7].

26. To this pertains what He said: "I went out from My Father and I came into the world," to be sure, not by shifting location but by taking for Himself a new and lowly nature [John 16:28].

27. He also left His mother Mary, since He put the whole church before His mother by teaching her and dying for her.

---

14. *mysticae historiae.* See Zanchi's comments on his historico-mystical interpretation of Genesis 2 in the first paragraph of this chapter (cf. note 2).

For that reason, He said to His mother and to Joseph, "Did you not know that I must be about My Father's business?" [Luke 2:49]. And again, "Who is My mother and who are My brothers?" [Matt. 12:48].

28. But Christ is joined to His wife by really and truly uniting His flesh with ours by the bond of His Spirit, so that every day, more and more, we might be made (and we are being made) one flesh with Him and He with us.

29. Adam indicated how very exclusive is the bond between Christ and the church when He spoke these words: "They shall be (two— according to Christ's interpretation) in לבשר אחד, *lebasar 'ekhad*" [one flesh; Gen. 2:24; cf. Matt. 19:5].

The apostle says, "This is a great mystery, but I am speaking of Christ and the church" [Eph. 5:32].

30. It was, therefore, a prophecy of the most exceedingly exclusive and indestructible union of Christ with the church and of the church with Christ.

31. There are, in Holy Scripture, infinite testimonies and examples and analogies of this true and real union by the Spirit of Christ.

32. The Son of God willed to reveal this union in His own person when "the Word was made flesh" [John 1:14]. Nothing more exclusive can be imagined than this hypostatic union of our nature with the divine nature in the person of the Son of God.

33. By this, as in a mirror, He predicted what and how great would be our future union, whereby He willed to become one flesh with the whole church, that is, with all of the elect and faithful.

34. There are in Christ two natures in one person; in us, many persons but with one nature or being, as it were. This is so both because Christ has taken on our flesh and also because we are made "partakers of His divine nature" [2 Peter 1:4]. Thus, Adam said well, "They shall be (two) in one flesh" [Gen. 2:24].

35. And furthermore, as Paul teaches, with Christ we are, as it were, "one new man" [Eph. 2:15] and one body, Christ the head and we the members.

And what could be more one? Is not the union between head and body true and real?

36. Christ also refers to this union when He says that He is the vine and we are the branches [John 15:5]. Does not a real union exist between the branches and the vine? Surely! So real that the vine itself and its juices really flow into the branches.

37. He also intended to describe this same union when He compared Himself to bread, which we eat, and the faithful to the eaters. For food consumed becomes one flesh with the one who consumes it. "He who eats My flesh…abides in Me, and I in him" (John 6[:56]).

38. He indicates the same thing when He says in John 17, "Keep them, Father,…that they might be one, just as We also are" [v. 11]. And again, "I pray that they (believers) all may be one, just as You, Father, are in Me and I in You; that they also might be one in Us" [v. 21].

39. The Father, Son, and Holy Spirit are three persons, but one in essence; we also are many, but we are one in Christ—one in essence, as it were. The persons are really distinguished between themselves, but, by reason of their essence, they are also really one and the same, that is, they are the one God. Not everything harmonizes in this comparison. Yet, by it is plainly shown what and how great is this union whereby, on account of our marriage, we become one flesh with Christ our Bridegroom.

40. Christ, moreover, is God of God, Light of Light, God the Son from God the Father. Likewise, we are flesh of flesh, bone of bones. Flesh, I say, and bone from Christ's flesh and of Christ's bones.

But elsewhere I have addressed this union more effusively.

Therefore, by this union He desired to prefigure the marriage of every man and woman. And Adam spoke of it in particular when he said, "For this reason a man shall leave his father and mother and shall cleave to his wife and they shall be (two) in one flesh" [Gen. 2:24].

### The Quality of the First Estate wherein Adam and Eve Existed

Finally, Moses briefly described the estate and condition of Adam and Eve now married, before sin. They were, he says, "both naked, Adam and his wife, and they were not ashamed" [Gen. 2:25]. First, they really were naked, and they went about naked. Second, their innocence is indicated by the words "they were not ashamed."

41. The spiritual marriage of Christ with the church in the wake of sin adopts this twofold condition. First, Christ always was and is naked from every sin. Likewise, He was naked, that is, poor, and was so for our sakes. For "being rich," says the apostle, "He became poor, that we might be rich" (to wit, with spiritual blessings) [2 Cor. 8:9].

Naked He came into this world. He was born naked. Naked (that is, poor) He lived. Likewise, He hung naked on the cross. And He took no earthly thing with Him when He ascended into heaven. Thus, this second Adam was naked also.

42. His wife also is naked. For, first, the church, being married to Christ, is laid bare and stripped of the old man, the earthly and carnal man—and daily more and more, until she is finally crowned with glory and honor like her Bridegroom and is presented in all her glory to her Bridegroom in the heavenly kingdom.

43. Moreover, she is largely naked of the blessings of this world. For this is the lot of the godly and of Christ's church, that just as our Bridegroom was poor in this world, "having nowhere to lay His head" [Luke 9:58], so also are we compelled to relinquish the blessings of this world for Christ's sake, to live in poverty, and to bear many persecutions and miseries. As many as want "to live godly in Christ shall suffer persecution," says the apostle [2 Tim. 3:12]. And we read concerning some of the apostles that "leaving everything, they followed Him" [Luke 5:11]. And "except one leave his house, lands, and everything that he has, he is not worthy of Me," says Christ [Matt. 10:37; 19:29; Luke 14:33]. Therefore, they were both naked—Adam and his wife, Christ and the church.

Moses goes on to say, "And they were not ashamed" [Gen. 2:25].

44. Christ was not ashamed of His nakedness, which He took up for our sakes. Nor, likewise, is the church ashamed, nor are any of the faithful, of His nakedness and poverty, which we suffer for the sake of our Bridegroom. Neither are they ashamed of the crosses and miseries that they are compelled to bear for the sake of the gospel of Christ.

45. The apostle says in 2 Timothy 1, "For which cause (that is, on account of the gospel that he preached) I also suffer these things (namely,

many miseries and chains), but I am not ashamed" [v. 12].[15] Likewise, in the same chapter, he praises the family of Onesiphorus because, for the apostle's sake, "he was not ashamed of my chains" [v. 16].

46. This, then, is the condition that accompanies those who truly, on account of their spiritual union with Christ, are one flesh with Him: naked they advance in this world, stripped of all their own righteousness, merits, and confidence in the flesh; largely they are stripped of this world's blessings as well. But they are stripped in such a way as not to be ashamed of their nakedness for Christ's sake.

This is the fourth thing that we have in that history concerning Christ's union.

Thus, from Moses's history of Eve's creation and her marriage with Adam we understand, to some extent, what is the church's creation and of what sort is her marriage with Christ. This, then, is how Paul's statement must be understood: "We are made flesh of Christ's flesh and bone from His bones" [Eph. 5:30]. And this is how, by means of this spiritual union, those two—Christ and the church—are made one flesh. As it says, "On this account a man shall leave father…and they will be two in one flesh" [Gen. 2:24]. And thus far the first chapter.

---

15. Zanchi strengthens the connection between 2 Timothy 1:12 and Genesis 2:25 by following the *Biblia Sacra* of Tremellius and Junius, which uses the verb *erubesco* (ashamed) in both passages, whereas the Vulgate uses *confundor* (perplexed) in Genesis 2:25. Zanchi, the Vulgate, and the *Biblia Sacra* agree in using a form of *erubesco* in the translation of 2 Timothy 1:16.

# Chapter Two

# The Doctrine of Carnal Marriage

The substance of the doctrine of carnal marriage, which began with Adam and Eve, and continued among the rest of mankind, and continues to the end of the world

We must hold firmly to this foundation, which we have already laid: just as two Adams—the first and the second, the earthly and the heavenly—are established by the apostle as two first principles[1] of humankind, one according to the flesh, the other according to the Spirit, so also, from the very history of Moses, he establishes a twofold marriage: a first and a second, a carnal and a spiritual. One is merely for men propagating in this world, and the other is for filling the kingdom of heaven with sons of God. For, as was explained above, the apostle gathers both of these marriages from Moses's own words.

Moreover, we have said something about both marriages in the first chapter—as much as Moses's history required—by comparing the one with the other using Moses's own narrative.

What we said concerning both of them collectively in the previous chapter we must now explain for each one separately and at greater length. First, in this second chapter, are propounded those things that we must know about the carnal marriage and then, in the third chapter, those things concerning the spiritual. For the true and natural method of teaching these things is, without doubt, to proceed from what we know better to what is less well known, from those things that descend to our

---

1. *duo prima principia.*

senses to those perceived by reason, from corporeal things to spiritual things, from types to the things themselves.

But we must both explain and demonstrate those things that are to be learned specifically about carnal marriage from Moses's history, as though faithfully drawing them up from the true and certain fountain of this whole doctrine, with a brief and logical method, according to the order of causes, duties, and consequences. And we proceed thus for this purpose: so that thereby, as was said above, what will subsequently be said concerning spiritual marriage may be more easily understood. Now on to the matter—but first to the explication of a few theses about carnal marriage that proceed from Moses's history that remain unexplained.

**Theses from Moses on Carnal Marriage**

1. Moses relates that out of all the animals not one was found that could be given to Adam as a helper, and therefore it was necessary for Eve, that she might be given to him in marriage, to be fashioned from his rib. From this we learn that it was contrary to God's will, and therefore contrary to nature, for man to have relations with beasts, which later was also decreed by law that it not be done (Lev. 18[:23]).

2. Furthermore, that God gave the woman to him also indicates that it is against nature, an abominable thing, for him to have sexual intercourse with a man, which later God both punished severely and expressly condemned in His law as deserving of capital punishment (Lev. 18[:22]).

3. Because God gave a wife to the man, he is to have sexual relations only with her. Thereby God declared that He condemns all wandering lusts and defilements, namely, any sexual activity outside the bounds of legitimate marriage.

4. Moreover, in what Moses said—that God brought Eve to Adam—he teaches that it is illicit for either a man or a woman to give himself or herself to someone else merely to satisfy his or her lusts, but only to him or her to whom he or she is called and given and to whom he or she has been joined by the Lord. And those who are united by the Word of the Lord are said to be united by the Lord.

5. Again, in God first requiring Adam's consent and then giving Eve to him, we learn that no man ought to have a woman forced upon him against his will and, by consequence, no woman a man against her will.

6. Since the Lord Himself brings the wife to the husband, we learn that it is illicit for spouses to divorce without the express will of God. For "what God has united, let not man separate" [Mark 10:9].

7. Whence also is gathered that whenever a woman marries legitimately and according to the Word of God, she is given by the Lord. Therefore, she is to be loved and cherished. For the Lord brought the woman to the man, and Solomon says, "House and riches are given by parents, but a prudent wife is from the Lord" (Prov. 19[:14]). So, let him who seeks a wife pray to the Lord that He may bring him a good wife.

8. Next, from what Adam said when he received Eve as his wife—"This is my bone and my flesh, of my bones and of my flesh" [Gen. 2:23]—we gather that it is the husband's duty to love and cherish the wife, just like his own flesh. "For no one hated his own flesh" [Eph. 5:29].

9. And from what Adam said—"For this reason, each one will leave father and mother and cleave to his wife" [Gen. 2:24]—in addition to what was said above, we also learn that in the contracting of marriage certain degrees [of consanguinity] must be respected. We also learn that we must take into account both blood and natural respectability, lest, in the first place, marriages be contracted with one's parents or with those who act in the place of parents. Hither comes that rule: Marriage between ancestors or descendants is never licit, and that is the case not only by the direct line but also by the oblique, and of course that includes those who are in the place of parents, whether by affinities or by consanguinities. Moses later spoke clearly and at great length about these degrees in a sweeping law (Lev. 18[:6–18]).

10. Polygamy is also condemned because God joined only two people—one man and one woman.[2] This follows Christ's interpretation of the passage: "And they will be two in one flesh" (Matt. 19[:5]). Similarly, he "will cleave to his wife"; therefore, not to his wives [Gen. 2:24; Matt. 19:5].

---

2. Zanchi follows Calvin and others in disapproving of the polygamy of the patriarchs. See Almond, *Adam and Eve*, 159.

11. With these words is adultery also condemned. He says, "He will cleave to his wife." Therefore, he shall not cleave to the wife of another or to her who is not his wife.

12. This passage also stipulates against divorce as long as your wife is yours or your husband is yours, for it says, "He will cleave to his wife." Therefore, as long as your wife is your wife, you shall not abandon her or turn her away from you. On the contrary, she remains your wife, if she has not committed adultery. And this is also what Christ concluded based on those words.

13. But if your wife either stops being one flesh with you and becomes one flesh with an adulterer, or if she refuses to have you cleave to her but instead abandons you, then you are free. Christ drew the first of these conclusions and the apostle drew the second [Matt. 19:9; 1 Cor. 7:15]. But it is always understood, first, that the cause must be legitimately known. For that saying of Christ must always be retained: "What God united, let not man separate" [Mark 10:9]. Therefore, if spouses must separate, they must come to God in His Word that He might separate them. Thus, they are only truly separated who are separated for a legitimate cause according to the Word of God.

As we will see, these things also pertain in a certain manner to the spiritual marriage, which is our focus. But now, in an orderly fashion, let us gather together and explain in some fixed and short theses those things that are and can be affirmed here and there about carnal marriage.

**Theses on Things Affirmed about Carnal Marriage**

In every marriage, these things must be considered in order—both with regard to the first marriage and also with regard to the institution of marriage as described by Moses.

1. The material cause
2. The efficient causes
3. The formal cause
4. The final causes
5. The duties of the wife and the husband
6. The consequences of marriage

*The Material of the Union*[3]

1. The material of the union is the male and the female. For matrimony is defined as the joining together of male and female.

2. Yet, neither every female nor every male is legitimate material for a marriage, but only those that are of the same species. Moses indicates this when he describes how, out of all the animals, none was found that could be given as a help to Adam [Gen. 2:20], and, therefore, Eve was created from Adam's rib.

3. Furthermore, neither is every woman nor every man suitable material for marriage. Rather, they must be adults so that they can consent to the marriage and so that they are prepared for the matrimonial duties. Thus, God created both Adam and Eve as adults and of a ripe age.

4. Neither is every adult man nor woman appropriate material. Rather, it is required that they be such as the law of the Lord prescribes in Leviticus 18[:6–18] with regard to the degrees of consanguinity and affinity. This same condition God indicated through Adam when he said, "He shall leave his father and mother" [Gen. 2:24], as explained above.

5. Also, in order for them to be legitimate material, it is necessary that they be just two: one male and one female and no more. For it is not that one woman is married to many men nor that one man can take many women in marriage. And the Lord teaches this as well—He joined just two people and gave the one woman to the one man.

6. He gave the faithful and pious woman to the faithful man. Therefore, in marriage, let care be taken that both of them are pious.

These, then, are the legitimate and appropriate material for marriage. And, therefore, the Lord created this material in the first place.

---

3. Zanchi draws upon Aristotelian language to structure his argument. Here and subsequently, he uses *materia* (material) to refer to the so-called material cause (*causa materialis*)—that which constitutes a thing. Zanchi will also speak of three other causes. The efficient cause (*causa efficiens*) is the agent that moves or changes a thing. The formal cause (*causa formalis*) is the shape or form produced in the material by the efficient cause. And the final cause (*causa finalis*) is the goal or purpose for which a thing is being changed or moved.

*The Efficient Causes*

In the second place, the efficient causes must be considered, that is, those things that create the marriage.

7. The first and principal cause is God, who instituted marriage, by whom the wife is given to the man and the husband to the woman, and by whom the laws of matrimony are established. Wherefore also Christ says that God is the one who joins: "What God has united, let not man separate" [Mark 10:9]. Thus, the consent of the divine will is the first efficient cause of the union.

8. But there are three more immediate causes: parental consent, the bridegroom's consent, and the bride's consent.

9. The parents betroth their children, and the children, once betrothed, consent to the betrothal. Thus, God, having first created the material of the union, then, immediately taking on the role of a father, desired that Eve marry Adam and that Adam receive Eve. And, first by the consent of God and then, afterward, of Eve and of Adam, the marriage was contracted.

10. Concerning the consent of the bridegroom and bride, there is no argument that without both parties' free consent there is no marriage.

11. But neither the law of God nor the imperial and Roman laws, which are derived from natural law, reckon any marriage to take place without the parents' will and consent. Therefore, as was said, there are three immediate causes that constitute a marriage: the parents' will, the son's voluntary consent, and the daughter's voluntary consent.

*The Formal Cause*

12. The formal cause of the union, which arises directly out of the three-fold consent, is the legitimate joining together of the two parties, by which the two become one flesh [Gen. 2:24].

13. For that is how marriage is defined: a legitimate joining together of male and female. The male and female are the marriage's material cause but the union itself is the formal cause.

14. For that is what happened with Adam and Eve. After they consented, they immediately became one flesh, and therefore he said, "This bone (surely, it is mine) and this flesh (surely, it is mine) is of my bones

and flesh" [v. 23]. And thus, he said of all marriages, "They shall be two in one flesh" [v. 24].

15. And Christ says, "What God has joined, let not man separate" [Matt. 19:6], teaching that just as the destruction of marriage consists in separation (meaning legitimate separation, that is, separation on account of adultery), so, by way of contrast, the constituting of the marriage consists in the joining together.

16. Thus, this joining together is the formal cause of marriage. For everything has its being by way of its form.

*The Final Causes*

17. The end is threefold: first, that man not be alone but rather have a companion and helper, and, in turn, that the woman not be alone, but rather have a man and head, a savior,[4] by whom she might be guided and protected throughout her whole life.

18. God indicates this end, saying, "It is not good for man to be alone; let Us make a helper for him, to be in his presence" [Gen. 2:18]. Thus, neither is it good for a woman to be alone, wherefore God gave the man to her as a head.

19. Nothing is happier than the life of the married, so long as those things are present that God wants to be in a true marriage—especially the union of souls, so that there is one soul in two bodies and, therefore, that they truly be one flesh. "For him who finds a good wife, she is more precious than jewels. The heart of her husband trusts in her and his estate will not diminish" (Prov. 31[:10–11]). Therefore, marriage was instituted in order that the life of man might be happier and more pleasant, because, in general, it was not good for him to be alone.

20. The second end is that there might be some offspring and legitimate heirs, by whom humankind might be propagated upon the earth and, consequently, from among whom the church, which will live eternally with Christ, might be gathered.

_______________

4. σωτῆρα: savior, deliverer, preserver.

21. For God wanted humankind to be propagated not by way of wandering lusts but rather by legitimate marriage, so that the elect might then be called forth and the church gathered from among them.

22. God expressed this end when blessing Adam and his wife. Thus, He says to them, "Be fruitful and multiply" [Gen. 1:28].

23. He also indicated this end with the word "built": "And He built the rib into a woman" [2:22]. For through the creation of Eve, who was to be given to the man in marriage, He signified that families, cities, kingdoms, and especially the church, would subsequently be built. It is concerning this also that Christ says, "And on this rock, I will build My church" [Matt. 16:18].

24. The third end was and is that, subsequent to the entrance of sin, wandering lusts and fornication might be avoided.

25. This is what the apostle teaches: "On account of fornication, let every man have his own wife" (1 Cor. 7[:2]).

26. Some add a fourth end, which is that carnal marriage is a mystery and sacrament of spiritual marriage.

*The Duties of the Husband and the Wife*

27. The duties of the husband and the wife ought to be considered here as well. These duties are the means, as it were, whereby the union is preserved. Of these there are two types: some are of both parties and some pertain only to one or the other.

28. The common ones are mutual love and mutual fidelity. For by love are the many united into one, because love joins the lover with the beloved, and by fidelity are all fellowships preserved.

29. Adam expresses both of these. The first, saying, "He will cleave to a wife" (not so much meaning bodily as soulfully and lovingly). The second, saying, "to his own wife," and again, saying, "They will be two in one flesh" [Gen. 2:24].

30. They should, therefore, keep this mutual fidelity with one another, not joining themselves to any other, lest they be made the flesh of another through adultery. By this very powerful means the bonds of matrimony are preserved.

31. The duties proper to each one are manifold, and I have spoken of them elsewhere. But in substance, they amount to this: that the wife be subject to her husband and depend on him and allow herself to be guided by him, and that the husband, as the head, guide his wife, cherish her, protect her, and keep her.

*The Consequences of Matrimony*
The consequences of matrimony must also be considered.

32. The first and primary consequence is that whenever one's body is made the joint property of another, everything that belongs to the one—both its prosperity and its adversity—are likewise made joint property to the other. Whatever belongs to the husband, let it be the wife's; whatever is the wife's, let it be the husband's. This is so characteristic of marriage and follows upon it so directly that it cannot be separated from it.

33. Moses demonstrated this, saying, "They shall be (two) in one flesh" [v. 24].

34. Second, there are various crosses and troubles amid which the state of marriage is practiced: poverty, death, exile, cares, injuries— suffered both at the hands of those close to home and at the hands of strangers. These must be endured in marriage.

35. Third, and on the other hand, there are also many consolations and blessings with which God affects the married who are living in true love and faith. For there is no lack of comforts and fruit in a pious and holy union. They are given children, their estate increases, they console one another in adversities, and in prosperity they rejoice with one another, and together they praise God.

To these few consequences of matrimony all others can be referred, even those that are usually numbered among the effects of matrimony.

Therefore, it appears that what has now been said regarding marriage according to its causes, duties, and consequences sufficiently encompasses the entire doctrine of marriage.

## The Significance of the Various Names of Matrimony

36. By way of confirmation, the various names used by the Greeks and the Latins to designate matrimony can be juxtaposed to indicate the various qualities and properties of wedlock.

37. The Greeks call it γάμον. There are two etymologies alleged for this word. Some want to say that γάμον is from δάμον, from the word δαμάζειν, "to dominate," because virgin women are dominated and subjected to men. This refers to the primary duty of the woman, which is that she be subject to her husband. Others prefer to say παρὰ τὸ δεδμῆσθαι ἀλλήλοις τοὺς συζύγους [that it is from "to be made mutually yoked together"] because the married are similarly bound together. This refers to the form. For marriage is the joining together of the two—the man and the woman. For they are ὁμόζυγοι [yoked together].

This second derivation corresponds in Latin to the word *coniugium*, from *iugum* [yoke], by which the two of them, male and female, are bound. This is why the apostle says, "Do not bear the yoke with unbelievers" [2 Cor. 6:14], that is, do not contract a marriage.

38. But *matrimonium* is so called from *mater* [mother], because to this end ought the woman principally to be married: that she might be a mother. And, so, Adam called his wife "Eve," הוה (*Havah*), meaning "life," because she would be "the mother of all the living" [Gen. 3:20]. This refers to the end of marriage.

39. They also called it *nuptiae* and *coniugium*, from *nubendo* [covering], because when virgins are led to marriage, they veil themselves for the sake of modesty and so that they might bear witness to their submission to their husband. We have the example of Rebecca in Genesis 24[:65].

Let this suffice for the second chapter, which concerns carnal marriage and which we, therefore, described in six parts.[5] We have done this so that, as we understand what has been said concerning carnal marriage, we might thereby equally well understand what will be said concerning spiritual marriage and what is taught about it throughout the Holy Scriptures—for we will follow the same method.

---

5. The "six parts" mentioned here refer to the six subheadings under the "Theses on Things Affirmed about Carnal Marriage." Zanchi describes spiritual marriage according to the same pattern in chapter three.

# The Doctrine of Spiritual Marriage

The doctrine of spiritual marriage is explained according to the pattern of the doctrine of carnal marriage

Let us come, then, to the third principal chapter and see how what we have said concerning the carnal union with regard to the types of causes may accord with the spiritual union, which is between Christ and the church.

## The Material of the Spiritual Union

*First Condition*

First was the material of the union, which is the male and the female—but not simply, for they must also be of the same species and nature.

1. In this spiritual union, on the one side is Christ in the place of the male, and on the other side is the holy church in the place of the female—in Eve's place, who was created of Adam's rib.

2. For Christ, the second Adam, is the church's head and her σωτήρ, from whose side the church was taken, according to the sense in which we explained above.

3. For He makes the church fruitful by the implantation in her soul of the seed of His word and by the Holy Spirit. Therefore, He deservedly occupies the role of the husband.

4. Truly the church has the role of the female and the wife, for she is subject to Christ, receives from Christ the spiritual seed, and with her help Christ begets for Himself many sons. Thus much concerning the first condition of the legitimate material in this spiritual marriage.

*Second Condition*

5. As for the second condition, Christ and the church are of the same species, on account of and according to the humanity He assumed.

6. For it was for this reason that the Word was made flesh, that is, the Son of God was made man so that He could be the church's true Bridegroom. For it would not be appropriate for this marriage to be contracted between persons who were not of the same species and nature, just as no one's head can be of a different nature and species than his body.

7. But, as Paul says, "Man is the head of the wife," and the wife is the husband's body and flesh [Eph. 5:23, 28].

8. So, properly speaking and according to Scripture, God is not the church's bridegroom, nor is the Holy Spirit, but rather the Son, for He alone was made man. Rather, the Father gave this bride to the Son, and through His Spirit bound her to and joined her together with the Son.

9. John 6[:37]: "All that the Father gives to Me." And, thus, John the Baptist says that Christ is the church's Bridegroom [John 3:29]. And the apostles also confirm this everywhere. Paul says, "I betrothed you to one husband, to present you as a virgin to Christ" [2 Cor. 11:2]. And in Revelation, the bride calls out to her Bridegroom and says, "Come, Lord Jesus! Come!" [Rev. 22:17, 20].

10. Wherefore also, whatever testimonies are read in the books of the Old Testament concerning the marriage between Jehovah and the church—such as that in Hosea 2[:20], "I will betroth Myself to you in faith"—they should all be properly and specifically understood of Christ, that is, of the Son manifested in the flesh.

11. For this is the reason—namely, so that He could be the church's true Bridegroom and of her same nature—the Son of God was made man, so that He might by nature be made like us in all things except for sin. And again, in order that the church also might be like Him, He regenerates her and cleanses her from all sin, so that the body differs not from the head nor the head from the body, but rather that both the husband and the wife might be one flesh, of the same nature and quality.

12. In this—that is, in this condition that stipulates that the bridegroom ought to be of the same species and nature as the bride and should be like the bride in all things, sin excepted—it is easy to see what

we should make of the doctrine of those who teach that the church has the kind of bridegroom whose body is utterly dissimilar to the body of His bride—invisible, impalpable, uncircumscribed, corporeally ubiquitous, and present in its substance.[1]

13. Such a one's body is certainly not the same kind as His bride's body. Such a Christ, therefore, is not her Bridegroom since He is not by nature like her in all things.

14. Therefore, he who subjects himself to this pseudo-Christ, whoever worships, adores, and cherishes him as his spouse, he commits adultery against the true Christ, who was made like us in all things except sin.

15. But, they say, it is the body of the same Christ that is circumscribed, visible, palpable in heaven yet invisible and so forth on earth.

16. I respond, in the first place, that the Scriptures do not describe such a Christ to us, nor did the church know such a Christ; no, indeed, contrary to Marcion, she rejected it.[2]

17. Either it is that same body or another that is said to be invisible and so forth. If it is a different one, then that Christ is not the church's Bridegroom, for the church's Bridegroom has a body and a soul of the same nature as the church's body and soul, that is, like us in all things. Again, the true Christ, the church's Bridegroom, has only the one body, which He obtained from the virgin and which is like ours in every way.

18. But if you say it is one and the same body but that it exists in different modes in heaven and on earth—circumscribed in heaven but ubiquitous in a definitive and omnipresent way in the bread,

---

1. For a discussion of the philosophical background from which terms like "uncircumscribed" and "corporeal ubiquity" emerge and the theological context in which Zanchi deployed them, see Stefan Lindholm, *Jerome Zanchi (1516–90) and the Analysis of Reformed Scholastic Christology* (Göttingen: Vandenhoeck & Ruprecht, 2016), 113–83. Suffice it to say, Zanchi is challenging a specifically Gnesio-Lutheran understanding of the relationship between Christ's human and divine natures.

2. Marcion (fl. 140) was an early and influential Gnostic. He argued that the physical world was created by a lesser god and therefore contemptible and unworthy of the God and Father revealed in the New Testament. See Tertullian, *Adversus Marcionem: Books 1–3*, ed. and trans. Edward Evans (Oxford: Clarendon, 1972), 196–97 (*ANF*, 3:328–29).

19. I respond, in the first place, that it is not possible for one and the same body to have so many modes of being.

20. Second, this also will follow: that body is not like ours in all things.

21. For never and nowhere was there, is there, or can there be such a bride's body that is both and at the same time visible and invisible, circumscribed and uncircumscribed, or that exists in a circumscribed way in one place but in a definitive and omnipresently ubiquitous way elsewhere.

22. So, neither can the church's true Bridegroom have such a body, since it has incompatible properties.

23. For, if it has them (notwithstanding that that is impossible[3]), it would not be the church's true Bridegroom, because it is not of the same nature and species as the bride.

24. In addition, that body—the one they say is ubiquitous, present but invisible, and so forth—is either animated and provided with a rational soul or not animated.

25. If not, then he who consists of this body is not the church's true Bridegroom, for the true Christ's body is animated and alive.

26. If it is animated, then it is either animated by the same soul that also animates that body, which is visibly and palpably in heaven, or else by another, different one.

27. If by a different one, then he is not our Christ, the church's Bridegroom. For our Christ consists of only one soul, just as also of one body. That one soul, I say, is the one that went out from His body when He died [Matt. 27:50]. And, hence, it was not at that time ubiquitous (for it was sent out from His body), so neither was it nor is it ubiquitous after being taken back up again.

28. But if you say that this invisible body is animated by the same soul as the visible body, which is in heaven, this cannot be true.

29. The first reason is because one soul cannot be the form of two completely different bodies.[4]

---

3. ἀδύνατον.
4. Here Zanchi draws upon the philosophical categories of form and matter.

30. The second reason is because our Bridegroom's human soul is the form of a physical, organic body. But the body that you imagine to be ubiquitous, uncircumscribed, and so forth is neither physical nor organic and so forth.

31. Again, the soul with which the body of our Bridegroom is provided, which is finite and circumscribed in heaven, does not exceed the bounds of His body nor does it surpass its substance. Therefore, the body that is invisible and corporeally present everywhere cannot be animated by that same soul that animates the visible body in heaven. For that reason, it cannot be our Bridegroom's body, since it is not of the same nature and species as the bride's body.

And let this suffice with regard to the second condition that is required in the legitimate material of this marriage.

*Third Condition*

32. The third condition of the material was that the man and woman be such as can consent to the marriage. This can be lacking neither in Christ nor in the church—in the church, I say, that is in adults (as is clear to all).[5]

33. Infants, however, although they cannot consent by an act of their own will, nevertheless do so by means of another's will—namely, by the will of the church and of their parents—which is to coincide with their own will when they reach maturity.

34. Accordingly, our heavenly Father, who has, by the blood of Christ and by the power of His Spirit, regenerated and grafted them into the body of the church, also claims them in the body of the church as Christ's flesh and does not exclude them from this holy union.

35. For the whole church is Christ's bride, and born-again infants are part of the church.

36. For although they, from their perspective, are said to become Christ's bride only when they themselves consent with their own will,

According to Aristotle every physical object is a compound of matter (here: the body) and form (here: the soul or animating principle).

5. Zanchi writes *adultis hominibus* (adult men), but he clearly means adults generally, both male and female, and uses "man" here inclusively.

nevertheless, as is said, Christ claims them as His bride—because He consents, because both their heavenly Father desires it in their name, and also their parents according to the flesh consent, and finally because He sees them consenting in their own time. That to which they now consent virtually[6] will in the end be recalled by act. Therefore, in this marriage, neither is the third condition of legitimate material wanting.

*Fourth Condition*

37. The fourth condition, concerning degrees of consanguinity, does not pertain and therefore presents no impediment.

*Fifth Condition*

38. The fifth material condition, namely, that there are only two—one male, one female—is not wanting.

For although the faithful (that is, the members of the church) are many and diverse, yet because they all are joined together into one by one and the same Spirit and baptized into one body by that same Spirit, the multitude of members does not, on that account, hinder them from being one body, one flesh, and, as it were, one man[7] and, so, one bride of Christ.

39. For neither does the multitude of members in the natural body of Christ hinder Him from having but one body. Nor are the two natures an impediment to His being just the one and the same Christ and, so, the one Bridegroom.

40. Rather, He is the one Christ because He is only the one person, consisting of one and the same deity with the Father and the Holy Spirit (that is, subsisting in one and the same essence), consisting likewise of one human soul and one human body, like ours in all ways.

41. Therefore, Christ—He who in His one and finite body is seated in heaven at the Father's right hand and whom alone the church always recognizes as her Bridegroom and no other—He, I say, is one.

42. Because, if you forge for Him another body and another soul,

---

6. δυνάμει.

7. *homo.* Zanchi may have Ephesians 2:15 in mind, where Paul describes Jews and Gentiles as "one new man" in Christ.

now the church will have not one Bridegroom, but two. But far be this polygamy from the church of Christ.

43. Thus, this condition also makes apparent how monstrous and blasphemous is the dogma of those who thereby give two bridegrooms to the church.

*Sixth Condition*

44. We raised a sixth condition that must be avoided: that a godly man not marry an ungodly woman nor a godly woman wed an ungodly man. For the apostle exhorts believers not to be yoked in marriage with unbelievers [2 Cor. 6:14].

45. Indeed, Christ first washed the church, which He desired to bind together to Himself, from her sins with His own blood on the cross, having clearly obtained for her the remission of sins from His Father and making her holy to Himself by the imputation and imparting of His holiness. Thereafter, by the washing of regeneration, He actually washes every single member of the church from sins and makes them holy with real holiness.

46. But as for those remnants of sins which still remain, some of them He does not impute to her, and some, more and more every day, he removes until she is finally established in heaven, all glorious and without spot or wrinkle [Eph. 5:27].

47. Hence it follows that they cannot be Christ's bride who are neither washed of their sins by Christ's blood nor reborn through His Spirit.

48. It was proper that she who was to be Adam's bride be created from Adam's own rib. So, it is necessary that she who is destined to be Christ's wife and bride be washed of her sins and regenerated from Christ's side, whence flowed blood and water. For the Father did not lead anyone to Adam except she who had been created holy out of his holy rib.

49. Nor did Adam recognize any other as his wife except she who had been taken from his rib. Nor did the wife know any other as her husband than he from whose rib she had been created holy.

50. Likewise, neither does Christ recognize any other as His church than she who was taken from His side on the cross, that is, who was washed of her sins by His blood and regenerated and made a new creation.

And, in turn, the true church knows no other as her Christ or husband but He who, according to the flesh, was born from the seed of David in the virgin's womb, who was in the cradle, who ate and drank with others, who did not live in every place among the nations but rather in Palestine among the Jews, who suffered for us, who was nailed to the cross, who gave up His spirit from His body, whose side was opened, from which emerged blood and water—truly the material of our redemption and regeneration. Accordingly, it is from His side, while He was dead on the cross, that the whole church was brought forth.

51. But out with it! This Christ whose body, say the heretics, is in its substance everywhere invisible and impalpable, is that He from whose side the church is made holy? For such a body has neither right side nor left side nor blood, nor is it of the seed of David, nor born of the virgin; neither did it suffer, nor was it crucified.

52. Therefore, Christ's church, just as it has never recognized such a Christ as its bridegroom, so neither should it now recognize such a one. It should be content with that Christ whose body is in heaven and by whose blood she is made holy and kept safe.

These, then, are the materials of the union. From these things it appears that if we bear in mind the union's legitimate material, then the true, legitimate, and holy union is the union between that Christ, who according to His human nature is in heaven, and the church, which is partly in heaven and partly on earth.

53. If anyone raises the exception of the angels—in that they are part of the church but, nevertheless, not of the same nature as Christ, being neither God nor men—to this I respond: First, on the basis of the apostle's testimony in Hebrews 12[:22], not to mention other places, I do not doubt that they belong to the body of the church. Second, while they are not men like Christ, nevertheless, on account of Christ's soul, they are not of so very different a nature. For just as it is a created spirit,[8] so they also are created spirits, furnished with intellect and will.

---

8. That is, Christ's soul, which as part of His human nature was, along with His body, prepared for Him by His Father and united to the eternal nature of the divine Son at the incarnation.

54. Nevertheless, properly speaking, the union is said to be contracted between Christ and the assembly of elect people.[9] For He did not take up angels (the apostle tells us[10]) into the unity of His person but rather the seed of Abraham. Nor can that which Paul preaches about Christ and the church truly be said of Christ and the angels, that they are "two in one flesh" or that they are "one flesh," since the angels are without flesh.

55. Nevertheless, they are both one with Christ and under Him as their Head. For Christ is also the head of the angels (Eph. 1[:21]; Col. 2[:10]). He is head over all principalities and powers, so grace and life and wisdom flow from Him to them, just as Christ also brings to pass in all faithful men. Accordingly, the angels cannot be separated from the body of the church. So, in a certain manner, they also are Christ's bride, although Scripture usually and plainly proclaims this only of the assembly of elect people.

56. The apostle in Ephesians 5 speaks only about that marriage of which the union of Adam and Eve was the type. But the union of which it was a type is that which is between Christ and the church, the assembly of faithful people.

**Concerning the Efficient Causes of the Spiritual Matrimony**

1. Next, I said that three efficient causes pertain, namely, a threefold consent—the parents' free consent, the bridegroom's free consent, and, in like manner, the bride's free and voluntary consent. And in our spiritual marriage, three consents are not wanting.

2. God the Father willed from all eternity that the Son, having taken our flesh into the unity of His person, might marry the church, that is, the whole body of the elect and that, in turn, the church might wed Christ and that the two might be made one body and one flesh.

---

9. Here (and in the following thesis) Zanchi again speaks of "men" but clearly intends the masculine noun to refer inclusively to the men and women who are elect in Christ.

10. The biblical reference here is ambiguous but probably is Hebrews 2:16.

3. Indeed, He first revealed and declared this as His will in the marriage of Adam and Eve, as in a mirror or figure (as the apostle explains in Ephesians 5), and consequently in all other legitimate marriages.

4. Again, by means of various promises about Christ and the church, He reveals in Moses and the Prophets that they should be united into one.

5. Nor was the covenant that He made with Abraham and his seed and that He frequently renewed with the fathers gazing elsewhere than at the covenant between Christ and the church.

6. But the Father made His will most splendidly manifest of all when, by sending the angel to Mary, He made known that He willed her to conceive a Son who would save His people, that is the church, from their sins and rule in the house of Jacob forever and be our Immanuel, so that He might be made one flesh with us and, thus, truly be God with us [Luke 1:31–33].

7. Finally, He revealed this as His perpetual will through the preaching of the gospel, that He desires that we be wed to Christ and be made one flesh with Him, flesh of His flesh and bone of His bones.

8. To this pertain the sacraments—baptism and the Supper—whereby we are received into fellowship[11] with Christ and grow together in Him. Therefore, the Father's will is sufficiently ascertained.

9. Now, the Son also willed from eternity the same thing as the Father and plainly made known His consent by the same means as the Father.

10. This was the voice of the Son to His church before He took on flesh: "I will betroth her to Me in faith" (Hos. 2[:20]).

11. In the Song of Solomon, however, He chose to describe this union with the church most beautifully. And, in Proverbs, eternal Wisdom (who is λόγος, the Son of God) says that His delight is that He be with the sons of man, that is, with His church [Prov. 8:31].

12. But, chiefly, He made known His will most fully to all when, taking on our flesh, He was made man, like us in all ways but without sin. He confirmed it with intimate companionship, kept company with us by diverse conversations, constant kindnesses and services, rejecting no one—not even prostitutes or publicans—so that He might draw all

---

11. κοινωνίαν.

to Himself through true repentance and faith, and incorporate them into Himself.

13. But how much more clearly and brightly could He declare that this was His will than when He voluntarily submitted to death for the church's salvation and shed His blood, whereby we are cleansed from sin and regenerated into a new creature?

14. For thereupon He promised and obtained the remission of the church's sins, her regeneration, and eternal union, whereby she might be made one flesh with Him and, finally, He acquired eternal life for her in His eternal and heavenly kingdom. "I will," He says, "that where I am, they also may be," those who believe in Me, that is, who will be My bride (John 17[:24]).

15. The apostle describes this will, whereby He willed that which the Father also willed concerning this marriage, in Philippians 2, where he exhorts, "Let this mind be in us that was also in Christ, who being in the form of God, did not consider equality with God to be robbery, but submitted Himself to Him…becoming obedient even unto death" [vv. 5–7]. And Ephesians 5, "Just as Christ loved the church and gave Himself for her…cleansing her with the washing of water in the word" [vv. 25–26].

16. He also makes this known as His will through the word of the gospel and seals it with the sacraments. Therefore, of the Son's will, and that most freely, there can be no doubt.

17. Yet, the Son has a twofold will: one divine, the other of His human nature. But both of them willed and continue to will this union with the elect. The one desired it from eternity; the other in time, which will never change and is the will of a created and finite soul that is one with its body in heaven.

18. The consent of the bride remains, for unless she—even each and every one of the faithful—freely consent to this union, it is not firm and established.

19. For (as stated above) a marriage is a legitimate joining together of one male and one female, proceeding from and contracted out of the free consent of both parties.

20. Hence, properly speaking, we say that this marriage is contracted with Christ when everyone consents by his own faith and his own will both to the Father's will (which commands that we recognize and embrace Christ as our Bridegroom) and also to the Bridegroom's will (which invites us to Himself and calls us through the apostles that we might be made one flesh with Him).

21. For that assertion made by the Son of God remains: "I betroth you to Myself in faith" (Hos. 2[:20]). And in John 3, John the Baptist, after he had declared Christ to be the church's Bridegroom [v. 29], encouraged faith in Him, whereby everyone might in themselves be joined to Him, as to a bridegroom, and live life eternal with Him: "For he who believes in the Son has eternal life but he who does not believe, the wrath of God abides on him" [v. 36]. And the apostle says, "I betrothed you to one husband, to present you a pure virgin to Christ" [2 Cor. 11:2]. How? By faith in the gospel, of course, whereby Christ offers Himself to us as Bridegroom and Savior.

22. Therefore, our consent is necessary for the contracting of this union with Christ Himself. For we are made one flesh with Him by faith, and therefore Christ is said to dwell in our hearts by faith (Eph. [3:17]).[12]

23. But whence comes this consent and free will? From the Father Himself, who draws us to Christ: "For He works in us to will and to accomplish according to His good will" (Phil. 2[:13]). For He caused the same thing to happen also that Adam and Eve might consent to their union.

24. But this consent cannot be in man except to the extent that he is now regenerated and made alive by the Holy Spirit.

25. For good consent cannot proceed from an evil, utterly corrupt, and distorted will. As Christ said, "An evil tree cannot bring forth good fruit" [Matt. 7:18].

26. Thus, it must be granted that to whomever true faith is given, in them regeneration has begun. As a result, it is subsequently more and more brought to completion through the increase of the Spirit. For what

---

12. The original mistakenly cites Ephesians 2 instead of 3.

dead man can do the works of life? But to believe in Christ and to consent to this spiritual marriage is a work of life.

27. Thus, as I said before, according to the order of nature, before a man can consent to this union with Christ with a true assent of faith, regeneration and renewal of the heart is first begun by the Holy Spirit, just as both Adam and Eve were first created and furnished with a living soul before they were joined in matrimony.

28. Therefore, these—the will of God the Father, the will of Christ the Bridegroom, and the willing consent of each of the faithful—truly and in and of themselves are the efficient causes of spiritual union.

## The Instrumental Causes

29. But the instrumental causes are the ministers of the gospel—as was John the Baptist, who called himself the friend of the Bridegroom and invited people to the wedding [John 3:29]; as also were the apostles, whence Paul: "I betrothed you to one husband to present you a pure virgin to Christ" [2 Cor. 11:2].

30. So then, each person has within him a sure testimony of this contracted marriage when he discerns himself to have been given true faith in Christ. This true faith is that by which he consents to the Father's will that he be made one flesh with Christ, according to His Word.

31. Still, this also must be noted: a certain knowledge of the person with whom the union is being contracted is required in the union. For mistaken identity ought to be absent from the union, lest you marry one person in place of another.

32. Therefore, each person must consent to union with the true Christ and be properly acquainted with Him and not to one whom he does not know with certainty from the Word of God to be the true Christ.

33. But the Holy Scriptures teach that He who is the true Christ, to whom the Father wills that we be joined by the bond of union, He is both true God, of the same essence[13] with the Father, and true man, like us in all things except sin.

---

13. ὁμοούσιον.

34. But nowhere do the Scriptures set forth a Christ who consists of an invisible, uncircumscribed, and everywhere-present body. Nor did the ancient church know or intend to receive such a one.

35. Therefore, let the faithful beware of a union with such a Christ whose body some imagine to be invisible, and let us be content with such a Christ as the Holy Scriptures set forth to us, as the Father revealed, saying, "This is My beloved Son" [Matt. 3:17]. Undoubtedly, He is the one whom John baptized and He is the one upon whom the Holy Spirit visibly descended in the form of a dove.

36. Surely, the Father did not reveal the sort of Christ who had an invisible body, nor upon such a one did the Spirit descend, nor was such a one baptized by John, nor did the blood and water whereby we are cleansed flow from such a body.

37. Furthermore, Jerome's letter to Pammachius against John of Jerusalem includes among the heresies the claim that, after the resurrection, Christ's body became invisible.[14]

38. So, such a monster and unnatural thing, begone! And let our bridegroom be Christ, of the same essence[15] with the Father and of the same essence[16] with His mother and like us in all things except sin.

## Concerning the Formal Cause of the Spiritual Marriage

In the spiritual union and in the third place we said that the formal cause must be considered, that is, the joining together of Christ and the church into one flesh.

Concerning this union, on which everything else in this treatise depends, these four things must be considered:

First, what things are made one? Is merely our soul (without our body) united with just Christ's soul? Or is our flesh also united with Christ's flesh and, so, our whole person with Christ's whole person?

---

14. Jerome, "To Pammachius against John of Jerusalem," 9 (*NPNF2*, 6:429). Jerome (347–420) was a church father most famous for the Latin translation of the Bible known as the Vulgate, which made the Old and New Testaments more easily accessible by making them available in the common language of the Roman Empire.

15. ὁμοούσιος.

16. ὁμοούσιος.

Second, if our whole person is united and made one with Christ's whole person, it is asked, Since Christ consists of a divine and a human nature, with which of these are we first united? With the divine or with the human?

Third, what type of union is this? Is it substantial or is it accidental, taking place only in the imagination?[17]

Fourth, if it is real and substantial, then how does it happen? Does Christ's body invisibly descend? Or is it that the substance of the air is transformed into Christ's body, so that by drawing in the air we are drawing in His body? Or is it really in the air and so is made one with the faithful? Or is there some other account?

*Explanation of the First Question*
As for the first, let this be our thesis:

1. Neither is our soul alone united with Christ's soul alone nor is our flesh alone united with Christ's flesh alone. Rather, the whole of every faithful person is truly united with Christ's whole person and coupled by the bond of this spiritual union and joined to Him.

2. The first reason is derived from the union of Adam and Eve. Adam's whole person was coupled with the whole person of Eve. Therefore, the whole of every faithful person is truly united with Christ's whole person.[18]

For that carnal union was the type of this spiritual union. That which was done carnally between them will without doubt exist spiritually between Christ and the church.

3. The apostle clearly teaches that when it was said, "They will be two in one flesh" [Eph. 5:31; cf. Gen. 2:24], this pertained to the mystery

---

17. The distinction between a substance and its accidents is derived from Aristotle. A substance is that which makes a thing what it is (i.e., that which makes a chair a chair; its "chairness"). By contrast, accidents are the qualities and quantities such as color, size, and location (i.e., the red chair, the big chair, or *that* chair over there) that might remain the same or even change over time. The question here is whether the church is united to Christ in substance or merely in accidents.

18. The original sentence reads "Therefore, etc." (*Ergo, &c.*), leaving the conclusion unstated but implied.

of the spiritual marriage between Christ and the church and must be understood concerning Christ and the church [Eph. 5:32].

But the word *two* signifies two persons, two human beings. Christ is one man and one person, and each of the faithful is the other person. Truly in Scripture the whole church is accepted as one person and one man, as was seen above and as the apostle clearly teaches in Ephesians 2[:15]. Therefore, in this spiritual union, the whole person of each of the faithful—namely, soul and body—is united together with the whole person of Christ and made one with Him—one flesh, one man.

4. Moreover, the text of Moses says, and so is cited by Paul, "A man will leave his father…and he will cleave to his wife" [Gen. 2:24; Eph. 5:31]. But a man is not just a soul. Nor is he just a body. Rather he is both together. Nor does a wife consist merely of a body nor of a soul alone but rather of both together. Just so, by the title *man* the apostle understands *Christ* in this spiritual union, and by the title *wife* he understands *the church*, and hence every one of the faithful. Therefore, that this might be a true union, it is necessary that the whole person of the faithful be united together with the whole person of Christ and that they grow together into one.

5. Christ Himself showed this beforehand when He was made man. For the whole person of the Son of God assumed in His unity the whole man, that is, the whole human nature, not just the flesh alone nor the soul alone but rather both together. Therefore, also, when He is made one with each of the faithful, the whole is made one with the whole.

6. Because Christ is the Bridegroom, He is for that reason also called by the apostle the Head and Savior of the church, because He disperses life and salvation to the church, as to His body and each one of His members. And Christ is neither the Head nor the Savior of the church only according to His divine nature, nor only according to His human nature, body and soul. Rather, our Head and our Savior is the whole Christ—in His deity, His soul, and His flesh. Neither is the soul alone of the faithful nor the body alone subject to Christ, but rather both, that is, the whole faithful man. But no one is made a partaker of salvation except through union and being fit together. Thus, the whole man is coupled together with the whole Christ in this spiritual union.

7. But the specific question is not about union with His deity but about the union of our flesh with Christ's flesh, particularly while we are in this world and our flesh is on earth but Christ's in heaven. For that reason, I will supply special testimony concerning the union of our flesh with Christ's flesh. Therefore, let this section containing these testimonies be the sixth argument:[19]

The apostle says in Ephesians 5, "We are members of His body (that is, Christ's), bone of His bones and flesh of His flesh" [v. 30]. Truly, he says this on account of our joining together with Christ. Again, "No one ever hated his own flesh, but nourishes and cherishes it" [v. 29]. Again, when it is said, "They will be two in one flesh" [v. 31], this is understood to refer to Christ and the church on account of the union that she has with Christ. Therefore, the apostle meant that we are made one (not only in soul but also in flesh) with Christ, not only with His deity or soul but also with His flesh, notwithstanding that it is in heaven. The apostle undoubtedly meant that we are truly united so that we become one flesh with Him. Likewise, in various places he mixes in the word *body*, saying, "We are one body with Christ."[20] And about the human body, the apostle says, "From its head, life flows into the members."[21] Again, to the Corinthians, he says, "Our bodies are Christ's members. Shall I then take the members of Christ and make them members of a harlot?" [1 Cor. 6:15]. John 6[:53]: "Unless you eat the flesh of the Son of Man…you will not have life in you." These and other similar testimonies witness most brilliantly that the union we have with Christ is not only of soul with soul nor even of flesh with deity but also of our flesh with the flesh of Christ, not with that Christ whom the heretics imagine to be

---

19. Zanchi's reference to a "sixth argument" is perplexing, since he does not clearly indicate which were the previous five. It seems likely, however, that he has in mind the immediately preceding sequence of theses, which offered various arguments demonstrating that "every faithful person is truly united with Christ's flesh." That would suggest that the first argument is contained in thesis 2, the second argument in thesis 3, the third argument in thesis 4, the fifth argument in thesis 6, and the sixth argument in thesis 7.

20. It is not clear to which texts Zanchi is referring here but it could be a paraphrase of Ephesians 5:30, which he quoted previously, or 1 Corinthians 12:27.

21. Again, the citation is unclear. Perhaps it is a paraphrase of Ephesians 1:22–23; 4:15–16; or Colossians 2:19.

invisible and immense and uncircumscribed. For how could we be one flesh and one body with that, since there is no similarity between our visible, finite, circumscribed flesh and that invisible one? Therefore, we are one flesh with Christ—not with that counterfeit flesh, nor are we united with it but rather with that which is in heaven and which is like ours in all ways, in substance and in nature.

8. The fathers bequeath the same doctrine. To produce the testimony of all of them is unnecessary. For, as I said before, all of them agree with Holy Scripture, especially with the word of Christ in John 6, "Unless you eat the flesh of the Son of Man…you will not have life in you" [v. 53]. Again, "He who eats My flesh…abides in Me, and I in him" [v. 56]. Again, according to the words of the apostle, "The bread that we break is fellowship[22] in the body of Christ" [1 Cor. 10:16]. That is, it is the thing whereby we are received into communion with the Lord's body and grow together into one. Accordingly, all the fathers, to a man, taught that in the Supper we eat the true flesh of Christ itself, namely, not that flesh imagined by heretics to be invisible and uncircumscribed but that which is like us in all things, sin excepted. And it is eaten in such a way that all of us, regardless of how many we may be, grow together as one with Christ, made flesh of His flesh and bone of His bones. Therefore, it will suffice to hear the testimony of one or two of the fathers.

9. Cyril of Alexandria, in his *Commentary on John*, clearly writes that Christ dwells in us by the communication of His flesh and we are His members on account of the words that Christ Himself spoke concerning His own flesh, "He who eats My flesh and drinks My blood abides in Me, and I in him" [John 6:56].[23] Cyril then goes on to say that "thereby we must consider that Christ is in us not only in disposition (by which is understood charity), but also by a natural participation."[24] But what does

---

22. κοινωνία.

23. Cyril of Alexandria, *Commentary on John*, trans. David Maxwell (Downers Grove, Ill.: InterVarsity 2015), 2:214. Cyril (ca. 376–444) was the patriarch of Alexandria, a prolific author, and a defender of orthodox Christology.

24. Cf. Cyril, *Commentary*, 2:214, which renders this passage as, "Here one may especially see that Christ says that he will be in us not by a mere relation understood in terms of disposition but by a natural participation." The reference to charity (*charitatem*) is, apparently, Zanchi's explanatory gloss.

he mean by "natural participation"? He certainly does not mean participation made by some natural means but true participation with Christ's natural flesh, whereby we are made and truly are one flesh and one body with Christ. Therefore, the word *natural* does not refer to *the means by which* we participate but rather to *the thing in which* we participate, that is, it must refer to Christ's natural flesh. Thus, the dream of invisible flesh is refuted, just as Cyril explained even more clearly, saying, "For just as if one mingles some wax melted by fire with other wax that is likewise melted, one thing is seen to be made from both, so by the communication of the body and blood of Christ, He is in us and we are in Him."[25]

10. An analogy, as they say, does not run on four feet.[26] For it is certain that neither our body nor Christ's body is melted in order that they might together be made one. Neither is there, therefore, any reason why anyone should imagine that Christ's flesh is here made one with ours through some physical contact, like wax with wax combined into one. For in that chapter and elsewhere, Cyril always clearly teaches that this union is effected by faith, as John 6 and Ephesians 3 teach. The apostle expresses this, saying, "That Christ may dwell in our hearts by faith" [Eph. 3:17]. But for Christ to be and abide in us [John 6:56] is the same thing as for Christ to dwell in our hearts. Moreover, the apostle teaches that He dwells by faith. Therefore, He is in us and remains in us and is made one with us by faith and, therefore, by faith also is He eaten. Wherefore, all physical contact must be excluded.

11. Nor, on the basis of this analogy of the wax, should we imagine some bodily presence of Christ, as if He cannot be made one with our flesh unless He is carnally and really present, just as the wax is present to the wax. For Cyril opposes and assaults this type of presence throughout his work, as do the other fathers. They are of the opinion that Christ's flesh (or Christ in His flesh) is in heaven and remains in heaven, and that He does not exist in the same manner on earth.

---

25. Cf. Cyril, *Commentary*, 2:214, which renders this passage as, "If one combines one piece of wax with another and melts them both with fire, one piece is made from both. In the same way, by participation with the body of Christ and his precious blood, we are united so that he is in us, and we are in him."

26. An ancient proverb meaning that no analogy holds equally well at every point.

12. Read that same Cyril in that same commentary explaining the words of Christ in John 17: "While I was with them, I kept them in Your name.… But now I am coming to You" (meaning, into heaven, for the Father is said to dwell in heaven) [vv. 12–13]. Cyril writes thus:

> The disciples supposed that Christ's absence—as a man, I mean, for God is everywhere present—would be the cause of many inconveniences to them since He was not present to be able to rescue them from all evils. But it was proper for them, who would become the lights of the world, to behold not only the flesh of Christ but also His deity, which although not perceived by the eyes, nevertheless is always present with the greatest degree of power, nor can anything hinder it from filling all things and from doing whatever it wills. For the divine nature is not circumscribed in one place or in dimensions (it is as if he had said, "like the human nature").

He adds:

> Wherefore, since Christ is truly God and man, they ought to understand that He will always be one with them by the power of His deity, even if He were absent in the flesh. For on that account He also previously said, "Holy Father, keep them in Your name, which You gave to Me," clearly indicating that they could be kept by means of His deity, not by the presence of His flesh.[27]

---

27. Cf. Cyril, *Commentary*, 2:287. Zanchi condenses this section of Cyril, which the modern translation renders as:

> The blessed disciples thought that our Savior's abandonment of them would result in great harm to them. (I mean his abandonment in the flesh—as God nothing can prevent him from being with whomever he wishes.) They thought that no one could save them once Christ had ascended into heaven. They would be exposed to those who wished to harm them, with no one to rescue them from the hand of their violent adversaries. Anyone who wanted to had the power to do anything to them and expose them to any danger without hindrance. Even though they were wise and fathers and lights of the world, we must not shrink back from saying that they should have looked not only at the incarnate presence of Christ our Savior but also should have realized that even if he were to deprive them of his presence with them in the flesh, and even if they could not see him with the eyes of the body, they should still surely have recognized that he is present and with them always by the power of his divine nature. After all, when will God lose his own attributes? What could oppose the nature that rules all things and get in the way, as if by force, preventing it

These all are Cyril's words, which he also explains more clearly in what follows in his commentary. Therein is contained also this idea, which should not be missed: Whatever things are proper to God cannot be performed by anything that is not substantially God. These are his words: "For nothing can do those things that are the works of God proper, unless that thing be God in substance."[28]

But to be everywhere present in His substance, is this not proper to God alone?

13. Let also chapter 22 be read, where Cyril emphasizes that Christ, insofar as He is man, is absent from us, but that He is present and fills everything only insofar as He is God.[29] From all of this it is clearly evident that by the analogy of the wax and by speaking of natural participation, Cyril hardly understood or intended to teach that Christ's flesh was made one with and communicated to us by bodily presence, nor by any carnal contact—whether visible or invisible—since he everywhere teaches that this is done by a spiritual presence, that is, by faith. It was in reference to this spiritual contact that Christ said, "Someone touched Me" [Luke 8:46].

14. What, then, did Cyril mean to communicate by the analogy of the wax? Nothing other than that just as the wax itself is incorporated into the wax to make one mass of wax from the two, so also are we incorporated into Christ Himself and, indeed, our flesh is incorporated into

---

from carrying out the activities that belong to it? Omnipresence is a God-befitting power and activity, ineffably filling heaven and earth, containing all things and being contained by none. God is not encompassed by a place or limited by distances or circumscribed within anything.... Therefore, since Christ is God and human at the same time, the disciples surely ought not to be unaware that even though he may be absent from them in the body, he will not entirely abandon them, but he will surely be with them according to his ineffable God-befitting power. That is why, it seems to me, that the Savior himself said, in the foregoing passage, "Holy Father, protect them by your name, that you have given me," in effect signaling to his disciples that the ability to save them was properly an activity of his divine nature, not of his presence in the flesh."

28. Cf. Cyril, *Commentary*, 2:288, which renders this passage as, "After all, he could not do acts that are proper to God without being in his essence what we understand God to be."

29. This is bk. 11, ch. 10 in Cyril, *Commentary*, 2:295–301.

Christ's flesh so that from the two is made one flesh. As it says, "They will be two in one flesh" [Gen. 2:24], which Paul understands as referring to the union between Christ and the church. So, Cyril's words should not be twisted to refer to the *manner*[30] *of the union* but rather must be understood as referring to *the things that are united*, that our flesh and Christ's flesh are truly and in themselves united—indeed, the whole of us with the whole Christ.

15. Rather, the manner is spiritual because this union and incorporation is by the Spirit of Christ and by our faith, as we will say later. And that the matter is thus, as we have said, is evident from a consideration of Cyril in book 10, chapter 13.[31]

For he wrote against those who said that by the word *vine*, of which we are the branches, should be understood only Christ's deity and, thus, that we are not ingrafted into Christ's true flesh but only into His deity. Cyril demonstrates that, on the contrary, albeit Christ's flesh is absent from us in heaven, nevertheless, we are truly and really ingrafted and incorporated into His true flesh. He proves this, chiefly, by the mystery of the Supper, where Christ holds forth His own true flesh to us to be eaten and says, "Whoever feeds on My flesh…abides in Me" [John 6:56]. But how is it eaten? By faith, just as Christ teaches in the same passage in John 6. For no distinction should be made between the way in which He is eaten and the way in which He is in us, since the reason He is in us is that He is eaten.

16. Just a little after the beginning of book 8 of *The Trinity*, Hilary of Poitiers[32] plainly teaches the same doctrine when he explains how the Father and the Son are one—namely, in the unity of nature and essence. There he also teaches that the unity whereby the faithful were and are one in Christ is assuredly accomplished by faith but is, nevertheless, natural because, as everyone knows, our natural flesh is united with Christ's

---

30. *modo.* Central to Zanchi's understanding of spiritual marriage is the difference between *what* is united and *how* the union is accomplished. For this reason, he emphasizes the manner (*modo*) of the union.

31. That is, bk. 10, ch. 2 in Cyril, *Commentary*, 2:210–17.

32. Hilary (ca. 300–368) was bishop of Poitiers and an opponent of Arianism in the Western church.

natural flesh. And, so, from the Lord's Supper, he draws that conclusion with these words: "As for what we say about the reality of Christ's nature in us, unless we have been taught by Him, we speak foolishly and impiously."[33] (Let those who argue about Christ's flesh and personal union—but do not do so from the words of Christ—note these words.) "'My flesh is true food, and My blood is true drink. Whoever feeds on My flesh and drinks My blood abides in Me, and I in him' [John 6:55–56]. Concerning the reality of Christ's flesh and blood there is no place for ambiguity: for now, both by the Lord's profession and also by our faith, it is true flesh and true blood. And these, being eaten and drunk, bring it to pass both that we are in Christ and Christ is in us. Is this not true? Those who deny that Jesus Christ is true God will conclude that it is not true. Therefore, He Himself is in us through His flesh and we are in Him, while together with Him we ourselves are in God."[34]

17. A little later, he calls this union we have with Christ a natural union, and he proves it, saying, "Moreover, how natural is this unity in us, He testified thus: 'Whoever eats My flesh and drinks My blood, I will abide in him and he in Me' [John 6:56]. For no one will be in Him save him in whom He will be; the only flesh that He takes unto Himself is that flesh which has taken His flesh."[35]

---

33. Cf. Hilary of Poitiers, *The Trinity*, trans. Stephen McKenna (Washington, D.C.: Catholic University of America Press, 1954), 286 (*NPNF2*, 9:141), which renders this passage as, "We speak in an absurd and godless manner about the divinity [*sic*] of Christ's nature in us…unless we have learned it from Him." McKenna's reference to "divinity" here is curious and may be a translation error—perhaps misreading *veritate* as *deitate*.

34. Cf. Hilary, *Trinity*, 286 (*NPNF2*, 9:141), which renders this passage as, "'For my flesh is food indeed, and my blood is drink indeed. He who eats my flesh and drinks my blood abides in me and I in him.' It is no longer permitted us to raise doubts about the true nature of the body and the blood, for, according to the statement of the Lord Himself as well as our faith, this is indeed flesh and blood. And these things that we receive bring it about that we are in Christ and Christ is in us. Is not this the truth? Those who deny that Jesus Christ is the true God are welcome to regard these words as false. He Himself, therefore, is in us through His flesh, and we are in Him, while that which we are with Him is in God."

35. Cf. Hilary, *Trinity*, 287 (*NPNF2*, 9:142), which translates this passage as, "He Himself thus testifies how natural is this unity in us: 'He who eats my flesh, and drinks my blood, abides in me and I in him.' No one will be in Him unless He Himself has been

Therefore, it is also clear from Hilary that our true and natural flesh is united in this spiritual union with the true and natural flesh of Christ, which we are discussing.

18. Leo I writes in this way: "For He does this by the participation of the body: that we pass into that which we lay hold of, that is, the flesh of Him who was made our flesh."[36] These are his words. Certainly, Christ was made our true and natural flesh. Therefore, we also pass into His natural flesh and we eat His natural flesh.

19. But how do we pass into His flesh? Not with bodily feet, surely? Or by transforming this flesh into Christ's flesh? Hardly. But rather by the Spirit and faith. Therefore, neither do we eat Christ's flesh with the mouth of the body. For we eat Christ's flesh in the same way by which we pass into it and by which means we abide in Him and He in us. For Christ unites both, saying, "He who eats My flesh abides in Me, and I in him" [John 6:56].

20. Now the sum of this is that just as we eat Christ's true and natural flesh, so are we made one with Christ's true flesh. And, conversely, just as we are made one with Christ's true and natural flesh, so also do we eat His natural flesh. These things are reciprocal.[37]

21. But when we are united with Christ's flesh and body, we are made a single body (as Cyril—or rather as the apostle to the Ephesians—says) with Him and one flesh.

Thus, from this certain and perspicuous doctrine is refuted that heresy of the ancient heretics, which seems to be recalled anew by some, concerning Christ's invisible, uncircumscribed, and everywhere-present flesh.

For, as Leo I says, we do not pass into that type of flesh. Nor are we made a single body with it, as Cyril (and, before him, the apostle) says. Nor are we made one flesh with it. Nor does Christ take it up into the unity of His person in the womb of the virgin. Nor was this flesh

---

in Him, while He has assumed and taken upon Himself the flesh of Him only who has received His own."

36. Leo the Great, "Letter 59: To the Clergy and People of the City of Constantinople," *NPNF2*, 12:60. Leo I was bishop of Rome from 440 to 461 and was a strong supporter of the Christology championed at the Council of Chalcedon, which met in 451.

37. ἀντιστρέφοντα.

crucified for us. Nor is it natural flesh, like ours. Therefore, neither do we eat it in the Supper, nor are we incorporated into it, but rather into that natural flesh (as the fathers say), which is in heaven.

22. Additionally, we are not made one with any but life-giving flesh. And this is the reason why we are made one with Christ's flesh, namely, that we might be made alive through it and live eternal life. Christ's flesh, however, does not make alive on its own, but only insofar as it was taken up by the Son of God in the unity of His person. But who dares to say that such flesh—flesh that has nothing in common with ours—was taken up by the Son of God into His person? Would this not be to deny that the Word[38] was made true man?

So, this first section that we undertook to explain the formal cause of the spiritual joining of our union with Christ is of no little consequence.

Wherefore, this doctrine should be diligently retained: In this holy marriage, the whole of us is united with and incorporated into the whole Christ and, indeed, our soul with Christ's soul and our natural flesh with Christ's natural flesh, which is, therefore, like ours in every way except sin.

*The Explanation of the Second Question*
The second question was: Since Christ consists of a divine as well as a human nature—Word and flesh—to which are the faithful first joined? To the human nature or to the divine?

This question is not asked without cause. For just as some (as we saw from Cyril) deny that we are united with Christ's human nature, as branches with the vine, but contend that we are grafted only into His deity, so also, among those who confess that we are coupled together with Christ's whole person, there are those who think we are first joined to His divine nature and afterward to His human nature (or, first to the Word and then to His flesh). Among other reasons, they think this because the Word comes nearer to us (since the Word is everywhere) than does the flesh, which is in heaven. But this is no reason. If this union were accomplished in a physical way, then it would have some bearing. But nothing impedes us, since the union is accomplished by the

---

38. λόγον.

Holy Spirit and by faith (as we will later explain). The Spirit makes us one with things that are distant as well as things that are close by, and faith also lays hold of that which is absent as well as that which is present. We can be joined to Christ's flesh as well as to the Word. Therefore, we should rather consider: In what order does God display Christ to us in the Scriptures and in what order does our faith lay hold of Him? Similarly, we should consider whether, first, our mind[39] is joined to Him and then, by consequence, our flesh? And whether to the Word or to the flesh?

This is our thesis:

1. A faithful man is joined first to Christ's flesh and then, afterward, through His flesh to the Word (or τῷ λόγῳ) Himself.

2. Here is a proof from the acquiring of knowledge. Just as with knowledge and mental apprehension, so also with voluntary unity and joining. For the will follows upon knowledge. It chooses, wills, embraces, and unites itself to something only insofar as one also has knowledge of and sees that thing clearly. For it is always drawn to the good—not the unknown but the known. And we lay hold of and know Christ as He is set forth in the Word of God first and most easily as man rather than as God. Therefore, by a certain order of nature and of actions—of the mind and of faith—we are, in the first place, made one with Christ's flesh and, through it, with His very deity and therefore with His whole person.

3. We easily prove this proposition[40] from Holy Scripture.

When, at the world's beginning, God promised a Redeemer, He immediately thereafter promised and displayed Him as the seed of the woman, that is, as a man. Genesis 3[:15]: "Her seed"—that is, the woman's—"will crush your head." Thus, to Abraham: "In your seed shall all the nations be blessed" [22:18].

Thus, Moses says, "He will raise up a prophet from among your brethren" [Deut. 18:15]. Thus, the Son Himself immediately displayed Himself to be seen by the fathers in the form of a human body and then,

---

39. *mens*: mind, heart, soul.

40. *assumptionem*. In logic, the *assumptio* is the minor proposition of a syllogism. The *assumptio* here is that the Scriptures first display Christ as man and then as God.

later, He declared himself to be the Angel of Jehovah—Jehovah Himself. Thus, the prophets prophesied and displayed Him first as man—as the seed of David—and then as Jehovah.

First, "Behold, the virgin will conceive and will bear a son." And, second, "And he will be called Immanuel" (Isa. 7[:14]). So also, "Behold, the days are coming, and I will raise up the righteous Branch for David." And after that he adds, "And this is the name by which they will call Him: Jehovah Our Righteousness" (Jer. 23[:5–6]).

Run through the Prophetic Books and you will see that Christ was always shown forth by the prophets in this same order—and, by way of the prophets, to the church.

The Evangelist Matthew does the same thing.

For, first, Christ is displayed as man, the son of Abraham and the son of David. Then, finally, citing Isaiah's prophecy, he calls Him Immanuel, and interprets it, saying, "That is, God with us" [Matt. 1:23]. Mark does the same, and so does Luke, who diligently describes Christ's whole genealogy as man and then, afterward, shows Him also to be God by miracles and other arguments.

4. If you object that John begins with Christ's deity, saying, "In the beginning was…" [John 1:1], and at length gets to His humanity, saying, "And the Word was made flesh" [v. 14], there is a prompt response. He did it for this reason: because the other Evangelists were more focused on describing His human nature. Indeed, it was because they showed Christ to be the Messiah, the son of David who was promised by the prophets, that John—content with the doctrine the other Evangelists had abundantly revealed, which they received from the fathers concerning Christ's human nature—summed up His incarnation in a single word, having first revealed His true and eternal deity.

Nevertheless, when he speaks about the knowledge of Christ, John shows that both he and others knew Him first as man and then, afterward, as God. For thus he says, "And He dwelt among us"—as man, of course—"and we beheld His glory" [v. 14]. "We beheld," that is, we have known on the basis of miracles and other testimonies and effects.

And John teaches the same thing in his epistle: "What we have seen and heard and our hands have handled, concerning the Word of life" [1 John 1:1]. Thus, they first knew Him as man and then as God.

In Romans 1[:3–4], the apostle maintains the same order, and he teaches that this is the order of the gospel he preached, saying he was set apart to the gospel of God, which He had promised beforehand concerning His Son. Which Son? First, he says, "Who was made flesh according to the seed of David"—behold, Christ as man—"but declared the Son of God…according to the Spirit of holiness"—behold, Christ as God. And it is certain that He was made man for this reason, to have Himself declared first to be man and then, subsequently, the only begotten Son of God and, so, God. And, thus, the apostle says in 1 Timothy 3[:16], "God was manifest in the flesh," that is, first He declared Himself to be flesh, that is, true man. Subsequently, He manifested Himself through His flesh and in His flesh to be God. And, therefore, he adds, "He was justified in the Spirit."

5. Wherefore, there is no doubt that such an order of foretelling, describing, displaying, and disclosing Christ was maintained in Holy Scripture—by the Father, prophets, Christ Himself, the Evangelists, and the apostles—so that knowledge of His human nature might first precede and then, afterward, knowledge of His divine nature might follow. But if that is the order whereby we come to know Christ and to lay hold of Him with our minds—the same order whereby He is displayed by the Holy Scriptures—then it is clearly evident that Christ first comes to the minds of faithful men as man and then, afterward, as God. And, hence, by faith are we also first made one with His flesh, which we initially lay hold of, and then, afterward, with His deity by way of His flesh.

6. No one can be united with God except by way of a mediator. Christ is that mediator not only as He is the Son of Man and true man but also as He is the Son of God—true God of true God. Nevertheless, His human nature taken up into the unity of His person is that whereby Christ was made the mediator and wherein He chiefly fulfilled the duties of mediator and whereby He declared Himself to be our mediator.

7. So, it is chiefly with regard to Christ's human nature that the apostle says, "The mediator between God and man, the man Christ Jesus"

[1 Tim. 2:5]. There he calls Christ the "man" the mediator *par excellence*,[41] because He fulfilled the duties of the mediator in human flesh.

8. Therefore, just as we are not united with God except by a mediator, so also, we are not united with Christ's deity except by way of His flesh, wherein the office of the mediator was fulfilled.

9. This saying pertains to this argument: "No one comes to the Father except through Me" [John 14:6]. Again, when Philip said, "Show us the Father," He responded, "He who sees Me also sees the Father" [v. 9]. He spoke of Himself insofar as He was man—obviously, the human nature taken up into the unity of the person of the divine Word.[42] In that man, as in a mirror, the whole nature and goodness of the Father blazed forth.

10. Therefore, neither can we ascend to Christ's deity, which is one and the same with the deity of the Father, except by way of His flesh.

11. Just as no one ascends to God or is united with God except by way of Christ the mediator—and specifically by way of His flesh, as was just shown—so also, God imparts nothing to us except by way of that same mediator, and specifically by way of His flesh. And this is the reason: because also in His flesh was redemption accomplished, sin blotted out, the devil conquered, death overcome, and life eternal secured.

12. Therefore, although the whole of salvation and life depends on the fullness of the deity that is in Christ, nevertheless, it is not communicated to us except in Christ's flesh and by way of Christ's flesh. Thus, Christ says, "Unless you eat the flesh of the Son of Man, you will not have life in you" [John 6:53]. Again, "Whoever feeds on My flesh… abides in Me" [v. 56].

13. For His deity is like a fountain whence flows all blessings, life, and salvation. But His flesh and humanity are like the channel whereby we receive all these blessings and graces.

14. Therefore, unless someone lays hold of this channel and is united with it, surely, he cannot partake of the waters that flow forth from the fountain.

---

41. κατ᾽ ἐξοχήν.
42. τοῦ λόγου.

15. To this argument pertains what the apostle teaches in Romans 5, saying, "Just as by one man sin…so also by one man righteousness abounded to many."[43]

16. As the apostle says, that righteousness is God's own righteousness, for it is both *of* Him and *from* Him who is true God. But it is not communicated to the faithful except by way of the man and by way of His flesh. Thus, the words of 1 Corinthians 15[:21]: "By a man came death, and by a man resurrection of the dead." Again, this: "His blood cleanses us from all sin" [1 John 1:7]. Again, "He washed us in His blood" [Rev. 1:5]. And other similar passages.

17. Certainly, sin and death were propagated by way of Adam's corrupt flesh. So also, then, righteousness and life are communicated to us by way of Christ's sanctified flesh, inseparably united with the eternal deity in the unity of His person.

18. God was not accustomed to give His responses nor hear prayers nor communicate His grace, except *out of* the ark of the covenant and *by way of* the visible ark and *by way of* that visible mercy seat. But in the ark lay hidden mysteries.

19. Christ's flesh is the ark, in which all the fullness of deity dwells bodily [Col. 2:9]. By way of it and from it are all the heavenly blessings displayed and communicated to us.

20. Therefore, just as it was necessary for the people to draw near to the visible ark and there to wait on God's graces, so no one may hope to receive God's grace unless he draws near to Christ, the visible man, and eats His flesh and takes it into his body by way of faith.

21. Wherefore, it is clearer than the noonday light that no man can become one with Christ's deity unless he is joined to His humanity and His flesh. For Christ's flesh is the instrument of deity—but assumed into and joined to the unity of the person.

22. This whole doctrine shines forth in the sacraments, as in a mirror most bright.

---

43. Zanchi does not quote directly from Romans 5 but rather combines elements from several different verses (vv. 12, 15–16, 18) into a composite quotation.

23. There are two things in a sacrament: the visible sign and the invisible grace, the earthly thing and the heavenly. He who draws near by way of faith receives both.

24. But in what order? In the same order in which God displays them: we perceive the thing signified by way of the sign and the heavenly thing by way of the earthly thing. For by way of the one, God offers the other.

25. Therefore, as by some divine order of dispensing, the sign is perceived and then, in the sign and by way of the sign, the thing signified, so, if you desire to become a partaker of His grace, you must first be made one with Christ's visible flesh and, subsequently, by way of it, with His deity. "Whoever feeds on My flesh…" Again, "Unless you eat…" (John 6[:54, 53]).

26. Hereby is also refuted the madness of that invisible flesh.

In order for someone to have life in himself, it is necessary that he eat Christ's flesh—*that* flesh, I say, which was taken up into the unity of His person. For no other flesh makes alive and this flesh makes alive for no other reason than because—and insofar as—it was taken up into the unity of the person of the Word.[44] But flesh that is invisible, and so forth, was not taken up into the unity of His person. For, if it were, then Christ was not true man, like us in everything yet without sin [Heb. 4:15]. Therefore, that flesh could not make us alive.[45] Wherefore, let this counterfeit and invisible flesh depart. It is necessary that we give no place to it. And let us be made one with His true and visible flesh, which is the only way whereby all heavenly treasures, salvation, and life are communicated to us.

The use of this doctrine is not meager. It is this: let us, in the exercise of faith and piety, fix the eyes of our mind immediately and initially on Jesus Christ's human flesh, as on the veil through which entrance is made into the Holy of Holies, where the glory of God shines forth, and

---

44. του λόγου.

45. Here, the translation fills out a particularly elliptical section of the treatise, which literally reads, "But flesh that is invisible, etc. was not taken up, etc. For, if it were, then Christ was not true man, like us in everything, etc. Therefore, etc."

then let us, as it were, enter into the Most Holy Place itself to behold His deity.

*The Third Question: What Sort of Union Is This?*
This question depends on the previous ones. However, it is put forward against two types of people. First, against those who think that this union is not true and real but only imaginary, because it is only done by a certain mental apprehension, just as we also comprehend in the imagination and with the mind other things and substances by way of intelligible forms and have them in our mind, but not because we are actually made one with them. The other type of person concedes that this union is true and real, but in no other way than because he is made a partaker of Christ's spiritual gifts and graces apart from the communication of the substance of Christ's flesh, just as we are also united with fire or with the sun merely by participating in the heat. Against each opinion, let this be our thesis to the proposed question:

1. Our union with Christ and of Christ with us is essential and substantial, true and real.

2. It is substantial because the very substances of Christ's flesh and of our flesh, of Christ's person and of our persons, are made one. But it is not merely that we gain the fruits that come from Christ, for they cannot be gained without gaining the substance of Christ Himself.

3. Moreover, we call the union true and real because we are not made one merely in our imagination but rather actually with Christ and, united, we grow more and more into one body. In its manner, however, the union is not physical but spiritual and supernatural, as we will say later.

4. All of this is clear, first, from the analogy with the carnal union used by the apostle: "They will be two in one flesh" [Eph. 5:31]. The union of husband and wife is certainly substantial because two persons are made one. Moreover, it is true and real because they are united into one true flesh and they are always one flesh. How? By reason of the conjugal bond with which they are bound together by the ordinance of God.

5. From that analogy this also may be inferred: while Christ's flesh may be in heaven and ours on earth, nevertheless, the physical distance

hardly hinders our true and real joining with His flesh. As also while a husband may be in the marketplace and the wife in the home, this distance of location does not hinder them from always being united as one flesh or, indeed, from being one flesh.

6. Second, the apostle also clearly explains that this union is essential, true, and real by means of another analogy that he uses in that same fifth chapter of Ephesians and frequently in other places, namely, of the head and members. He says Christ is the head of the church; we are His body and members [Eph. 5:30]. Obviously, the union of the members with the head and among themselves is substantial, true, and real.

7. From that analogy let us also understand that we cannot receive the fruits of Christ's suffering and His gifts and grace except by real participation in Christ's flesh. For neither can the members, if separated from the head, enjoy motion, life, energy, or nourishment.

8. Third, the same thing is confirmed by the analogy of the living foundation and, likewise, of the living stones built upon the foundation, who, on account of their real and truly substantial conjunction with the foundation, continually increase until they grow into a holy temple in the Lord [Eph. 2:20–22; 1 Peter 2:4–5].

9. To this pertains the fact that Christ more than once referred to Himself as the foundation upon which He builds His church (Matt. 16[:18]).

10. Fourth, Christ described this same real conjunction and incorporation with the analogy of the vine and the branches. In John 15, He says, "I am the vine, and you are the branches. Just as the branch cannot bear fruit of itself, unless it abides in the vine, neither can you, unless you abide in Me" [vv. 4–5]. What is clearer from this analogy than that we are truly and really grafted into Christ?

11. What the apostle wrote in Romans 11[:17], concerning the olive tree and the branches grafted into it, pertains as well.

12. The same doctrine is confirmed because Christ described this union with the phrase "feeding on His flesh and drinking His blood." John 6[:56]: "Whoever feeds on My flesh."

He who eats and drinks, does he not become one—substantially and really—with that food and drink? Yes, certainly! And in such a way that one substance is made from the food eaten and the one eating the food. Nor can food and drink convey life, unless they are, in their substance, really made one with the eater and drinker.

13. Hence, Cyril and other fathers said that Christ dwells in us corporeally and naturally. We indicated a little earlier how these words should be understood, namely, not with reference to the manner[46] whereby Christ dwells in us, as if He were in us in a natural or carnal way. Rather, this concerns the thing to which we are united. For we are made one with Christ's true and natural body and, indeed, by a true and real union, but by way of the Spirit and faith.

14. For the fathers chose to conclude that we the faithful are not only made one with Christ's deity by the consent of the will and by a certain condition (as the heretics said), but also with His natural flesh and body, and thus is our flesh nourished unto eternal life.

15. For the heretics said that, after His resurrection, Christ's flesh is no longer necessary, the mystery of redemption having been completed in it. And, hence, since it is no longer any use to us, it has, therefore, either disappeared or been transformed into deity.

16. Against this, Cyril and other fathers showed the perpetual usefulness of His flesh, chiefly from Christ's words in John 6: "Unless you feed on the flesh of the Son of Man, you will not have life in you" [v. 53].

17. They conclude, therefore, that Christ retains His natural flesh and that He impresses its power and, as it were, its image onto our flesh by communicating His sanctity to us, whereby we are made flesh of His flesh and bones of His bones. They also conclude that He brings us to His flesh by way of the Holy Spirit and, so, makes us alive by way of His flesh, and that nothing is communicated to us from the Father unto salvation except by way of Christ's flesh, truly and really communicated to us. And they succeeded in proving this, most particularly, from the mystery of the Lord's Supper.

18. For just as the bread is really and truly made one with us in our eating of it, so also, Christ's flesh is truly and actually made one with us who eat it.

---

46. *modo.*

19. Nevertheless, there is a great distinction in the way[47] whereby the corporeal food is eaten by the corporeal mouth and the way it is made one with us in a corporeal fashion. But we both eat and incorporate to us the spiritual (that is, the true) flesh of Christ spiritually. And we are, undoubtedly, joined to Him by way of[48] faith and by way of the Holy Spirit. This is what the fathers taught.

20. On the basis both of these passages and analogies from the Holy Scriptures, as well as from the testimonies of the fathers, I suppose that it is clear that our union with Christ is essential and substantial and true and real, so that we are truly made His one body, because Christ the Bridegroom and the church His bride are two in one flesh.

21. Whereby also is refuted anew the fiction of Christ's invisible and impalpable flesh. For the church is not one with such flesh but with that natural flesh that is in heaven. "The husband will cleave to his wife and they will be two in one flesh" [Gen. 2:24]. That is, Christ, in His natural flesh, is joined to the church and to the flesh of every one of the faithful, and so, by the force of this union, the two become one flesh. Thus, if they are one flesh, then the bride's flesh cannot differ in its substance from her Bridegroom's flesh.

22. But what likeness can there be between our visible flesh and that imaginary invisible flesh?

Therefore, also from this—that our union with Christ is substantial and real—is the point proven that there cannot be a union between us and this invisible flesh, but only with that flesh which is like ours in nature and substance, and which makes ours like unto itself in holiness and righteousness.

And let this suffice for the third question.

---

47. *modo.*

48. *per.* By repeatedly employing words like *modo* (manner) and the preposition *per* (by means of, by way of) Zanchi emphasizes the instrumentality of believers' union with Christ. Failure to properly discern that the union with Christ's flesh is spiritual (and not corporeal) leads to embracing a Christ other than the one who is the church's true and heavenly Bridegroom.

*The Fourth and Last Question: Concerning the Manner[49] whereby
This Union Is Established*

This union is established at the preaching of the gospel, in baptism, and in the Lord's Supper, for which reason there are also various responses to this question. Everyone confesses that, at the preaching of the gospel, the union is established by way of faith alone—that is, *effectual* faith. Neither is there much disagreement concerning the way whereby it is established in baptism. But, with regard to the way whereby we are made one with Christ's flesh and Christ's flesh is made one with us in the Supper, no one is ignorant of how many debates there are among those who profess Christ.

The Pontificals[50] demand that besides faith, we are also made one in a corporeal and truly physical manner, because, they say, the substance of the bread is transformed into the substance of Christ's body. And so, just as the accidents of the bread and wine are perceived by the eye and transferred to the belly, so also, together with them, the true substance itself of Christ's body is received with the corporeal mouth.

Those who follow Luther teach the same way of receiving—for although they do not concede a change of essence,[51] they nevertheless defend a mingling of essence.[52] So, they cannot teach anything other than receiving with the corporeal mouth. And, thus, they teach that this union is formed bodily, that is, in a corporeal manner. They also labor to confirm this, along with other arguments, with certain sayings of the

---

49. *modo.*

50. *Pontificii.* This derogatory term refers to those theologians who embraced the theology—in this case, specifically, the eucharistic theology—of the Roman Catholic Church.

51. μετουσίαν: transubstantiation.

52. συνουσίαν: consubstantiation. The following quotation by the influential Lutheran scholastic theologian Johann Gerhard (1582–1637) is instructive both because it clarifies what Protestants generally meant by words like μετουσίαν and συνουσίαν, and also because it signals the complex and divergent ways in which Lutheran and Reformed theologians could deploy such terms: "Briefly, we do not declare ἀπουσίαν (an absence), or ἐνουσίαν (an inclusion), or συνουσίαν (a mingling [*consubstantionem*]), or μετουσίαν (a transubstantiation), but rather παρουσίαν (a presence) of Christ's body and blood in the Lord's Supper." Johann Gerhard, *Loci theologici* (Frankfurt and Hamburg, 1657), 5:56.

fathers. But these are twisted and understood improperly, as with what Cyril said about John (concerning which see above; and this opinion is also followed by other fathers), to suggest that Christ dwells in us by His body naturally, corporeally, by natural participation. Indeed, the ubiquitarians endeavor to prove His ubiquity from that place in Cyril as well. But how shamelessly they misuse those sayings is clear from that place.

First, because all the fathers openly and constantly teach that Christ does not dwell in us according to the flesh, but according to His deity, that is, not by a carnal presence but by the presence of His deity. Again, "On account of His being man, He is in heaven, but on account of His being God, He is with us on earth until the end of the age."[53] And they always contrast the absence of Christ's body with the presence of His Spirit and deity. This will seem obvious to anyone who reads the fathers. Therefore, they never understood Christ's flesh to be united to us naturally and corporeally here on earth, that is, in a natural and corporeal manner.

Next, the places in Scripture that those fathers used to prove their pronouncement about the natural union with Christ plainly teach in what sense the fathers were thus speaking. The places are John 6[:56]: "Whosoever feeds on My flesh…" But there, with regard to the manner of eating, Christ expressly urged that it is by way of[54] faith and He condemned carnal feeding.

Another place is John 15[:5]: "I am the vine…." There also the manner is by way of faith.

Another place is 1 Corinthians 10[:16–17], concerning fellowship.[55] And there the apostle teaches that we have that same fellowship[56] with the whole body of the church that we also have with Christ, the head. But we certainly are not united with one another in a corporeal manner.

Third, the same is clear because the fathers teach that Christ is united to us and we are incorporated into Him as much in baptism as

---

53. Zanchi here paraphrases Augustine's letter to Dardanus. See Augustine, *Letters*, trans. Roland Teske, ed. Boniface Ramsey (Hyde Park, N.Y.: New City, 2004), 3:249.

54. *per.*

55. κοινωνίᾳ.

56. κοινωνίαν.

in the Supper. But, clearly, in baptism this union is not established in a corporeal manner.

Fourth, it clearly accords with what the fathers teach based on those against whom they wrote what they wrote. They did not write against those who taught that Christ was laid hold of and received by faith alone but rather against the Eutychians, who contended that Christ's post-resurrection flesh either disappeared or was absorbed into the deity, since now it was no longer of use to us. And, therefore, they said that we are only united with His deity and that He dwells in us only in His deity. The fathers taught, conversely, that Christ retained His flesh and that we are made one with it and that Christ dwells in us in His flesh, but by the bond of Spirit and of faith, yet the whole Christ dwells in us (Eph. 3[:17]).

Therefore, when they said that Christ dwells in us naturally and corporeally, that must not be understood as referring to *the manner* in which He was received but rather to *what* was received and that *by which* Christ dwells in us—namely, His natural and true body.

Therefore, let this be our thesis for the question:

1. The union whereby we are, in our flesh and soul, made one and bound with Christ in one flesh is formed by way of the Holy Spirit and faith.

2. In order that this might be rightly understood, what we said above regarding the efficient cause of the union must be remembered. For we said that it is properly contracted out of the consent of both parties, but we said that the union is the very joining together of the man and the woman, whereby two are made into one flesh (or are made one flesh). Christ effectually revealed His consent to us by pouring out His Spirit into our hearts. For, by the Spirit, He causes us to understand that He truly desires to be our Bridegroom and, so, our Head and Savior[57]—and that this is His Father's will as well.

3. On the other hand, we consent to this union with Christ by way of faith,[58] aroused in us by the Holy Spirit.

---

57. σωτῆρα.
58. *per fidem.*

4. And just as He makes us one with Himself by imparting[59] His Spirit, so we are joined to Him by way of faith. Therefore, this is what I previously said: this union is formed by way of the Spirit (with respect to Christ) and by way of faith (with respect to us).

5. Concerning the Spirit, in the fourth chapter of his epistle John says, "By this we know that Christ is in us, from the Spirit whom He gave us" [1 John 4:13]. Therefore, Christ joins Himself to us by way of His Spirit and enters our heart by way of that same Spirit. And the Spirit makes plain to us and causes us to know that He is in us and that we have been taken up into fellowship[60] with Him. And Romans 8[:9]: "Whoever does not have the Spirit of Christ, is not His." Therefore, we are made the members of Christ—truly, of the Bridegroom—and flesh of His flesh, by way of the Spirit, by whom He incorporates Himself to us and us to Him.

6. Concerning faith, in Ephesians 3[:17] the apostle says, "Christ dwells in our hearts by way of faith." Therefore, we receive Him into our hearts by way of faith as well and are made one with Him. And John 6[:56]: "Whoever eats My flesh and drinks My blood remains in Me, and I in him." But He is eaten and drunk by way of faith, just as Christ explained in the same place, saying, "Whoever believes in Me will never thirst" [v. 35]. Thus, we are made one with Christ by way of faith.

7. Wherefore, whether Christ is set forth in the Word or in baptism or in the Supper, He is always made one with us by way of His Spirit and by way of our faith, and we with Him.

8. Concerning baptism, the apostle says this: "For through one Spirit (ἐν ἑνὶ πνεύματι) we were all baptized into one body" (1 Cor. 12[:13]). Therefore, we are incorporated into Christ in baptism and we are made His members by the power of the Holy Spirit.

9. Concerning the Supper, in the same place, he adds, "And we all have been made to drink in one Spirit" (meaning, by the common experience in one Spirit[61]) [v. 13]. What does he mean by "in one Spirit"? He

---

59. *per communicationem.*

60. κοινωνίαν.

61. ἀπό του κοινού εν ενί πνεύματι. This interpolated Greek explanation appears to be drawn from Homily 30 (on 1 Cor. 12:12–20) of the great preacher and archbishop

means that just as we all are one body in Christ, so we all also live by the same Spirit. Therefore, by the power of His same Holy Spirit we drink Christ's blood in the Supper, and we grow together with Him into one, and we are made alive by His Spirit.

10. For just as all the members of a body are made one with the head by one and the same soul and are made alive, so all the faithful, although they may be on earth and their head in heaven, nevertheless, are really made one with Him by way of the one and the same Spirit. And, being united to Him, they endure and have life.

11. Nor did any of the fathers teach anything else. Augustine, in his fiftieth tractate on John, says, "Let them (the Jews) hear and lay hold of Christ, who sits at the right hand of the Father in heaven. The Jew responds: Whom shall I lay hold of? The absent one? How shall I reach my hand up to heaven, that I might lay hold of the one who sits there? Reach out your faith and you will lay hold. Your ancestors laid hold by flesh; you, lay hold with the heart, for the absent Christ is also present. Unless He were present, it would not be possible for us to lay hold."[62] Moreover, Augustine explains many times that Christ is absent in the flesh but also present in majesty.

12. Therefore, it is clearer than the light at midday that we receive Christ—His flesh and blood—by Spirit and by faith and that the whole us is joined to the whole Christ, and we become one flesh. So, lest our adversaries dare to oppose this account of the union, let us, content with this union, seek no other, because the Scriptures propound no other and because, just as this one alone is necessary for salvation, so also is it sufficient according to the agreement of all.

13. From all of this it is clear that if we regard that *to which* we are

---

of Constantinople, John Chrysostom (ca. 347–407). Cf. Chrysostom, *Argumentum Epistolae primae ad Corinthios, et Homiliae XLIV in eadem Epistolam*, vol. 10 of *Joannis Chyrsostomi Opera omnia*, ed. Theobald Fix, 2nd ed. (Paris: Gaume Fratres, 1837), 315 (*NPNF1*, 12:176).

62. Augustine, *Homilies on the Gospel of John*, trans. Edmund Hill, ed. Allan D. Fitzgerald (Hyde Park, N.Y.: New City, 2020), 2:129–38 (*NPNF1*, 7:279–80).

united or the truth of the union, then this union is essential and real. But if we consider the manner[63] *by which*, then it is spiritual.

14. Hereby is refuted that impious dogma of the invisible and everywhere-present flesh as well. For they contrived this flesh for this purpose: so that we could receive it with the corporeal mouth. But this is unnecessary. For, since all confess that we receive Christ by His true and natural flesh, which is in heaven, and are made one by way of Christ's Spirit and by way of our faith, what is the purpose of this other invisible and everywhere-present flesh except that it may be received by the *corporeal* mouth?

15. No indeed, not even by the corporeal mouth can the whole be received by even one of the faithful. For none of the faithful is everywhere, that he might devour the whole of this everywhere-present flesh. Instead, one little bit will be gotten by one person and another person will get another little bit.

16. By this same argument is refuted both the opinion of transubstantiation and of consubstantiation.[64]

For since Christ's flesh is received by the Spirit and by faith—and by them unto salvation—not only in the word of the gospel but also in baptism and in the Supper, both transubstantiation and consubstantiation[65] are superfluous. Why, therefore, trouble the church and fight over a thing that is unnecessary for salvation?

And let that suffice for the third chapter, in which were explained these four questions: (1) What things are made one? (2) With which thing are we first united, either Christ's deity (and, by way of it, His flesh) or His flesh first (and, by way of it, His deity)? (3) What sort of union is this? (4) How is it established?

---

63. *modum.*

64. συνουσία.

65. μετουσία and συνουσία.

# Chapter Four

# The Final Causes of the Spiritual Union

1. We said that there were three ends[1] for the institution of carnal marriage: (1) that man might not be alone but have a helper like unto him and, so, lead a happy life; (2) that he might thereby beget children; (3) that, after sin, he might be able to avoid all wandering lusts and fornications. One can behold all these ends in the spiritual union between Christ and the church.

## The First End

2. The first end was that it was not good. Just as it is not profitable for a head to be without a body nor a body to be apart from the head, so neither was it good for Christ to be alone without the church nor for the church to be alone without Christ.

3. Rather, it was determined from all eternity that this Christ would be the church's head, and rule her, and make her alive, and save her, and live with her in eternal happiness. And, conversely, the church was predestined to be Christ's body and to be ruled, made alive, and given eternal life by Him.

4. Therefore, both for Christ's benefit (because it pertained to His glory that this Man not live alone in heaven) and for the church's good (because this was necessary for her eternal salvation), God the Father created the church from the side of Christ while He was asleep on the cross (that is, dead) in the sense that I explained at the beginning of this

---

1. *fines*: that toward which a thing moves; its goal, purpose, or end.

treatise. And He gave her to the Son in matrimony, that they might live together most happily forever in the glory of heaven.

5. What the apostle wrote to the Corinthians concerning Christ's resurrection and the resurrection of the whole church through Christ to eternal life pertains to this. For after all things have been made subject to Christ, then will He also be made subject, with His whole body (that is, the church, His bride), to the Father, that God might be all in all (1 Cor. 15[:28]).

6. Therefore, Christ's glory and the church's salvation were the first end of this union. And, on that account, He loves her and cleanses and washes her every day, that He might finally establish her glorious unto Himself, having neither spot nor wrinkle nor anything else of that sort, but rather that she might be completely holy and innocent, and so that they might both live together happily in heaven.

## The Second End

7. The second end was (and is) that from the seed of Christ the Bridegroom—that is, from His word and Spirit—by way of the ministry and help of the bride, He might beget children, most numerous and beautiful, to be the heirs of the kingdom of heaven.

8. These are all of the faithful, since they are conceived from the spiritual and incorruptible seed in the womb of the church and by her ministry, and they are born the sons of God by the washing of regeneration and by the renewal of the Holy Spirit [Titus 3:5].

9. Indeed, it is not absurd that those same faithful are, in different respects, called both Christ's bride and the sons of God, and therefore, also the children of Christ and of the church.

10. As each one is regenerated and born a son of God from Christ's Spirit in the church and by way of her ministry, so he is the child of Christ and the church. But as each one is joined to Christ by way of faith for the receiving of His spiritual seed—the word and the Spirit— and for bearing the fruit of good works whereby he might win others to Christ, so he is the bride.

11. All the apostles and doctors and pastors were first the children of the church, because they were born by way of the church's ministry

from God and made sons of God. But as others were likewise reborn of water and the Holy Spirit by way of their ministry, so they were Christ's brides and the mothers, as it were, of the other faithful. And so the apostle calls himself the mother, as it were, of the Galatians, saying, "My little children, for whom I am in labor again" [Gal. 4:19]. And to the Corinthians, "I have begotten you in Christ" [1 Cor. 4:15].

12. Thus, the whole church is usually called our mother, since, in her and by way of her ministry, each one of the faithful is regenerated, nourished, and guided. Whence also the apostle in Galatians spoke of the Jerusalem above (that is, the church), which comes, as it were, from heaven, saying, "Which is the mother of us all" [Gal. 4:26]. For many interpret the passage thus, with regard to the church.

13. Thus, clearly it is not absurd for each of the faithful to be called Christ's bride and His children in different respects.

14. Wherefore also is demonstrated the second end of this spiritual union—that by way of the bride's ministry, spiritual children are daily begotten in the church.

15. Notwithstanding, another type of child was also appointed to this union, namely, the children of good works. For each one is joined to Christ, as bride, by way of faith. And Christ, as Bridegroom, is joined to each one of us by way of His Spirit so that, receiving His spiritual seed, we bring spiritual children forth into the light, that is, we produce the fruit of the Spirit and of good works.

16. For Christ does not want His word and grace to be idle but rather to grow and be made known abroad by good works to God's glory and the church's edification.

17. To this pertains also that passage from 2 Corinthians 6: "We appeal to you not to receive the grace of God in vain (or, with no effect)… causing offense in nothing" [vv. 1–3].

## The Third End

18. The third end was (and is) the avoidance of all fornication.

19. But there is a twofold fornication: one specific, the other general. The specific type of fornication is all idolatry, namely, fornication

with idols and with demons, concerning which the prophets speak throughout.

20. The general fornication is any sin whatever whereby we rebel against God and play the whore with creatures. Concerning this general fornication, Psalm 73[:27]: "You destroyed all those who committed fornication against You." For they are said to have committed fornication against God who did not persevere in obeying God's commands but fell too much in love with creatures and, neglecting God, invested their heart in them.

21. But everyone who is not incorporated into Christ by way of true faith, sins in both types of fornication.

22. Yet, both are done away with by a true union and holy binding with Christ the Bridegroom. For whoever remains in Christ will always have the Spirit from Christ, by whom he is restrained so that he does not serve the devil, sin, and his desires but rather seeks God alone and is zealous to do His will.

23. To this pertains that saying of Christ to the disciples in John 15: "Abide in Me, and I in you. Just as the branch cannot bear fruit by itself, unless it abides in the vine, neither can you, unless you abide in Me. I am the vine, and you are the branches. Whoever abides in Me, and I abide in him, he bears much fruit, for without Me you can do nothing" [vv. 4–5].

24. From this passage it manifestly appears that this union with Christ (or this spiritual union) was established for this end: to avoid all types of fornication and, conversely, that we might serve God with faith and obedience.

25. And it is certain that all who are truly incorporated into Christ by this bond of holy union conduct themselves in this way. For they are ruled by the Spirit of Christ, so that they walk not according to the flesh but rather according to the Spirit [Rom. 8:4].

26. What, then, must be thought of those who live perpetually in every kind of fornication? Certainly, they are not Christ's bride, and so neither are they the church nor members of the church. And let this suffice regarding the final causes.

# Chapter Five

# The Duties of the Husband and of the Wife

In the fifth place, it follows concerning the duties of the husband and of the wife, whereby both matrimony itself is kept whole and undiminished and also the spouses live happily together with one another.

## The Common and Proper Duties

1. We said that certain of these duties were common to both parties and that certain of them were proper to one or the other.

2. The common duties are mutual fidelity and mutual love.

3. The proper duties of the husband were restricted to this summary: that, as head, he rule wisely, justly exercise dominion, guide, cherish, nourish, protect, and serve his wife as his own flesh, and that he forgive her, as the weaker vessel, of many things.

4. But the proper duties of the wife are that, as her husband is her head, she should fear, revere, heed, and remain subject to him as her lord and savior,[1] that she should listen to him attentively and allow herself to be guided, that she not be insolent to him but rather simply obey him in the Lord with modesty, gentleness, and peace. For thus the apostle instructs both in Ephesians 5[:22–33] and in 1 Timothy 2[:9–15]; so also in 1 Peter 3[:1–7].

5. As pertains to Christ, what duty can be desired of Him that He has not discharged and does not continue always to discharge? The apostle says, "He loved the church and gave Himself for her, that He might sanctify her, cleansing her with the washing of the water in the

---

1. *servatorem*: savior, deliverer, preserver.

word, that He might present her to Himself glorious, having neither spot nor wrinkle nor any such thing" but rather that she might be holy and pure (Eph. 5[:25–27]). Again, "He it is who saves the body" [v. 23]. Again, "He nourishes and cherishes her as His own flesh" [v. 29]. Certainly, He remains faithful to the whole church and to each of her true members, even if not all of those who are in her remain faithful. "Does the faithlessness of those nullify the faithfulness of God?" (Rom. 3[:3]). Again, "If we are without faith, He nevertheless remains faithful; He cannot deny Himself" (2 Tim. 2[:13]). Who does not perceive and feel how great and how many are the things for which He daily pardons us as the weaker vessels? Therefore, Christ always executes the duties of the good—of the best—husband.

6. But with regard to the church's duties toward Christ—what they are and whether she does them—in order that this is rightly understood, the church, which is Christ's bride, must be distinguished from an adulteress. For the apostle speaks only of the bride and not of the adulteress, since he says that she submits to Christ [Eph. 5:24].

7. Therefore, when we speak of the church, we are excluding all reprobates and hypocrites, some of whom are in the church but are not of the church—just as feces also are in the human body but are not part of the body.

8. Thus, insofar as this matter is concerned, the true church, Christ's bride, is the assembly of the elect in which are, nevertheless, also found many hypocrites.

9. Next, this assembly must be distinguished within itself between those who are in heaven and those who are on earth. The former are usually called the church triumphant, the latter the church militant. And the former are the pure wheat, purged from all chaff, while the latter are wheat intermixed with much chaff.

10. By the word *chaff*, however, I mean not only hypocrites, who are intermixed with the elect, but also the remnants of sins, from which no one living in this flesh is entirely free and purged.

11. Therefore, in the third place, the church of the elect abiding on earth must be distinguished into the flesh and the Spirit. For every one of the faithful consists of flesh and Spirit.

This is the distinction of the bride into her parts. She is, indeed, only one bride and one body, but she consists of various parts and members.

12. Thus, the part of her that is in heaven certainly does all of the duties that can and should be done there. For she is truly and perfectly subject to Christ as Head and Bridegroom. So, there Christ and the church are truly and perfectly two in one flesh, living in the fullness of peace and in most perfect love—O happy marriage!

13. Moreover, I implore that this also be observed: What sort of doctrine is it whereby some say that Christ's flesh is invisible and everywhere present? Christ's church and bride certainly is only one, and that part of her which is on earth submits to that same Bridegroom Christ and, so, enjoys the same Bridegroom's body as that part of her that is in heaven, which submits to and enjoys that body which is also in heaven. For there is only one Bridegroom and His flesh is one, just as also there is one church.

And the church, insofar as she is in heaven, has Christ according to His finite, visible, circumscribed flesh. And she submits to that Christ—and to that body of Christ—and, therefore, she also enjoys that body and none other, which our opponents also concede. They say that Christ's body is circumscriptively in heaven, or that Christ is in heaven in a visible and circumscribed body, with the same proportions as our bodies.

Add that while the spirits of the blessed are innumerable, they nevertheless enjoy one and the same body of Christ and, indeed, each one enjoys the whole. Therefore, the same church, which is partly on earth, submits to the same visible and circumscribed body of Christ and enjoys that same body and not another.

14. Certainly, they cannot deny that the church on earth truly enjoys Christ's circumscribed body by way of faith. But no one denies that this is sufficient for our salvation in this world.

15. We say that the church, insofar as she is in heaven, can perfectly fulfill all of the duties that are to be performed there. But insofar as she is on earth, how does she behave herself?

16. Concerning this, the apostle says that she also submits to Christ, by which he means according to the Spirit. But according to the flesh she often forsakes submission and obedience. The apostle said, "In my

mind, indeed, I serve the law of God, but in my flesh the law of sin" (Rom. 7[:25]).

17. But because, in her principal part, she remains submissive and because, when she rebels according to the flesh, for His part the Bridegroom forgives that rebellion of His wife as the weaker vessel (as Peter says every good husband does toward his wife [1 Peter 3:7]), therefore, truly it is said that she who is now wholly submissive, albeit imperfectly, will submit perfectly in heaven.

18. And so we conclude that this marriage about which the apostle speaks is perpetual, never to be dissolved.

19. For a marriage cannot be dissolved except on account of fornication or on account of adultery. But this church does not commit fornication in the Spirit, and, indeed, she strives not to commit fornication in the flesh. For she says with the apostles, "Where shall we go? O Lord Jesus, You alone have the words of eternal life" [John 6:68].

20. Nevertheless, she often falters according to the flesh, as also when Peter denied Christ. But because faith did not falter in His heart, for that reason, with repentance aroused in Peter, there followed pardon from Christ his Bridegroom, whose duty is to love His bride and sanctify her, washing her from every stain of sin [Eph. 5:26–27].

21. But that we who are still occupied with the flesh might more clearly understand what our duty is toward our Bridegroom and that we may strive to do it, it should be observed that these are the principal duties signified by the word *submission*.

22. If the duty of the wife is to undertake to be submissive to her husband, just as the body to its head, then first we owe faith to our Bridegroom, whereby let us truly believe that Christ is our Bridegroom and we are loved by Him and that whatsoever He promises, He will fulfill. For no one freely remains submissive to him whom he mistrusts and by whom he does not believe he is loved.

23. Next, we owe delight joined with greatest reverence. For he who loves not cannot bear submission. But he who loves is not burdened in submitting to him whom he loves and respects.

24. Third, we owe conjugal fidelity, whereby the bride has bound herself to her husband alone. For this is chiefly what is signified by

the term *submission*. For she does not submit herself to another but to her husband.

25. Moreover, this duty follows from the first and second, for the woman who is both persuaded that she is loved by her husband and who, in turn, loves and obeys her husband will easily preserve the promised fidelity and remain in submission.

26. Fourth, we owe obedience in all things that the Bridegroom commands, to hear His voice, and to give heed to it. For true submission demands this too.

27. Peter explains this in 1 Peter 3[:1]. First, he says, "Let wives be subject to their own husbands." Then, a little later, he uses the example of Sarah to explain wherein this submission chiefly consists, namely, in obedience and reverence toward the husband, saying, "As Sarah obeyed Abraham, calling him lord" [1 Peter 3:6].

28. Fifth, from here follows the humility of soul whereby a good wife does not speak insolently to her husband or desire to have dominion over him or to rule him but rather permits herself to be guided by him and to be ruled by him and willingly carries out his commands.

29. This also is included in true submission. Therefore, the apostle explaining in 1 Timothy 2[:11–12] says, "Let a woman learn in silence, in all submission; for I do not permit a woman to teach or to usurp authority over men but to be in silence."

30. From here the sixth duty follows, namely, perpetual repentance. If we sin because of infirmity or out of ignorance, let us immediately, with the greatest humility of soul, run back to our Bridegroom and beg His pardon for our guilt. For true submission requires this, and it proceeds from true faith and delight and from a humble soul and spirit.

31. If we diligently strive to fulfill these things, we shall also for our part make this holy marriage honorable. And let us endeavor that it might be perpetual and that we might truly experience how sweet it is to be with Christ.

32. Add also this to the end: our duty is not to allow the seed of the word of God, and the gift of the Holy Spirit to remain idle in us. Rather, let us take care, each one of us according to our utmost ability, that every day we bear new sons to Christ by way of the word and Spirit.

## The Consequences of Spiritual Marriage

1. Indeed, who is able either to conceive with the mind or to explain with words the true pleasures and divine joys that accompany this spiritual union?

2. For they are both manifold and nearly infinite and also truly extensive and most abundant.

3. For Christ the Bridegroom is the maker and Lord of all things that are in heaven and on earth.

4. Moreover, whatever belongs to the Bridegroom, it all becomes common with the bride by right of the union, and, in particular, the house with all of its furnishing and servants, the table, and the bed. For it is so necessary that they dwell, spend their life, and attend to sleep and rest together that without these things the union cannot be complete.

5. For if, as the proverb says, "all things are common among friends"[2] (but only in their use; each one's property is reserved), how much more for those who are united together, since then their bodies are also made so common that there are no longer two but only one body, and they are made and truly said to be one flesh?

6. But all of the Bridegroom's belongings are of two types: some for life in the age to come, some for the present age.

7. Again, among those that concern the present age, some pertain to spiritual life, others to corporeal, or human, life.

## The Blessings of the Present Age

### The Blessings That Pertain to Corporeal Life

8. Those things that pertain to corporeal life are the heavens, the elements, everything made from the elements, and whatever can be assembled or made from them.

9. Indeed, I will speak first about this other, second type, of blessings. Of course, they are in many ways all ours and can truly be said to belong to us.

10. In the first place, they belong to us at least because of the right and dominion over the other creatures that was given to Adam before

---

2. πάντα τὰ τῶν φίλων κοινά.

sin. It is restored to us who are made one flesh with Christ in Christ Himself, our Bridegroom and Head. He said, "All power has been given to Me in heaven and on earth" [Matt. 28:18].

11. Next, in that same Christ, we not only have the right to all these things but also the complete and full possession of all things.

12. For Christ sits at the Father's right hand, and we, says the apostle, "are seated with Him in the heavenly places" (Eph. 2[:6]). Therefore, if the Bridegroom is also Lord over this inferior world, then the bride herself must also be its lady.

13. Third, as it pertains to each one of us (so to speak) in particular, while we do not always actually and really possess every single one of these blessings together, nevertheless, we have the right of possessing them when there is need, so that whatever things we use, we delight in them with a good conscience, as if we were using and delighting in our own things. And we can use and delight in them as ours in a way that cannot truly be said of those who are rich and powerful—even princes—yet wicked. And to this pertains that statement of the apostle, "All things are pure to the pure; to the unfaithful, however, nothing is pure, but their mind and conscience are defiled" (Titus 1[:15]).

14. On the other hand, the reason that we do not actually enjoy them all and at all times is because our most wise Bridegroom, the Lord Jesus—who neither hates nor neglects His own flesh but rather nourishes and cherishes her—knows very well either that we do not need them or that they would not be expedient for us.

15. Add to this that not only do we have the right to possess these blessings in this age but also that we really do possess them whenever we will. Indeed, if we are truly Christ's bride, then we will to possess whatever our most beloved Bridegroom desires us to possess and nothing else.

16. But we know that the Bridegroom wills that we possess only those things that He Himself provides for us. But He knows to provide those things that come to us without deceit, without wicked conduct.

17. But who can be said to be richer, more powerful, more blessed than he who can do whatever he wills to do and who has what he wills

and who is content with his lot? This pertains to what the apostle said, "But godliness with a soul content with its lot is great gain" [1 Tim. 6:6].

18. Finally, to whatever extent we may not directly possess in ourselves the things of this world, nevertheless, we do possess them in others, insofar as all things, by the Bridegroom's command, serve to promote our life and salvation.

19. To this, the apostle's statement can, not incongruously, be accommodated: "All things are yours, and you are Christ's, and Christ is God's" (1 Cor. 3[:22–23]). For all things—yes, even the things of this present age—are ordained unto our life and salvation, just as it is appointed to each one to live. But cannot all these things be observed in a carnal marriage, especially where the humble bride is most attentive to her husband and, conversely, where she is loved by her powerful husband? And let this suffice concerning these corporeal blessings.

Now, concerning those blessings that pertain to the spiritual life, they are imparted in this way.

*The Blessings That Pertain to Spiritual Life in This Age*
1. God established and confirmed all blessings in the one mediator, Christ, and specifically in His flesh, such that unless they are received[3] from Christ, as from a fountain, no one can partake of them.

2. Almost all the Scriptures, which declare that salvation must be sought only in Christ, have this in view. "God has given us…life, and this life is in His Son" (1 John 5[:11]). Indeed, in the word *life* is encompassed our entire salvation. Colossians 1[:19]: "in Him (namely, Christ) all the fullness was pleased to dwell." Again, John 1[:29]: "Behold, the Lamb of God, who takes away the sins of the world," and the infinite other passages of this type. By these passages is demonstrated that all the heavenly

_______________

3. *communicentur*. Here and in the sections that follow, Zanchi focuses again on the manner in which Christ and believers are united. This time he specifically considers how Christ communicates His blessings to His bride. This leads Zanchi to draw upon a constellation of Latin terms that emphasize instrumentality and manner—the *how* of the union—in order to shed light on what spiritual marriage means for those united to Christ by faith and Spirit both now and in the future.

and divine treasures were in the one Son of God made man, just as the apostle testifies in eloquent words in Colossians 2:3.

3. These treasures are truly communicated to them who are so made one with Christ that they are made one with Him—one body and one flesh.

4. For the apostle says, Christ is He who gives salvation to the body, namely, to the whole church, which is His body and flesh and to each one of the faithful who likewise are one flesh with Christ and bones of His bones.

5. But this union and incorporation cannot be formed except by way of the Spirit Himself and our faith, just as the Scriptures teach throughout.

6. Therefore, this communication of Christ's treasures truly pertains to the whole of the church, Christ's true bride, and to her alone and to each one of the faithful who are in her, who are given the Spirit of Christ.

*The Twofold Manner of Communicating*[4]
7. But this communication is twofold, namely, by way of imputation and by way of real communication.[5]

8. Christ the Bridegroom is, on account of the union, entirely ours along with all of His treasures, but the treasures are themselves infinite and most abundant. Therefore, they cannot be contained in us ourselves but must be communicated to us and made ours by way of imputation.

9. Moreover, these two manners[6] of communicating both the other blessings and, primarily, Christ's righteousness are so interconnected, as cause and effect that they are not separated from one another nor should we separate them, no more than the solar ray can really be separated from the sun or the sun from the ray.

10. For we learn from the Holy Scriptures that to whomsoever Christ's perfect righteousness is imputed, he is indeed also given that righteousness which they call inherent.

---

4. *ratio communicandi.*

5. *per realem communicationem.*

6. *rationes.*

11. What David said has this in view: "Blessed are those whose iniquities are forgiven and whose sins are covered. Blessed is the man to whom the Lord has not imputed sin, and in whose spirit is no deceit" [Ps. 32:1–2].

12. For the last clause refers to inherent righteousness, but the previous clauses refer to imputed righteousness. And the passage has tied both of them together, lest we suppose that the one can be separated from the other.

13. In fact, this is also how things normally work in marriage. For instance, whomever the king grants to become his bride and wife, to her he also normally presents betrothal gifts and royal ornaments to wear, so that she may thereby be distinguished from other women and known clearly to be the wife of such a king.

14. For it is not *because* she is adorned with royal vestments and precious stones that she is the king's wife. Rather, because she is the king's wife, *therefore*, she is adorned and provided with signs of royalty whereby it might clearly be seen by all just whose wife she is.

15. It follows from this that it cannot be determined truly and pronounced with certainty whether someone is or is not truly reputed righteous before God except on the basis of inherent righteousness and genuine fruit.

*The Communication of Blessings by Way of Imputation*
16. With regard to imputation, in the first place, there is the well-known passage in Romans 5: "Just as by[7] the disobedience of the one man (imputed to all who are born of Adam by natural generation) many were constituted sinners, so by[8] the obedience (imputed to all who are born again[9] of Christ's Spirit) of the one (namely, the man Christ) many are constituted righteous (namely, all of the elect)" (vv. 18–19).

17. "By the obedience of the one," says the apostle, meaning the *whole* of His obedience. For there are two parts to Christ's perfect obedience.

---

7. *per.*
8. *per.*
9. ἄνωθεν.

The one is that whereby He was obedient in keeping that whole law most perfectly, less for Himself privately than for all of us in common to whom eternal life was promised. The other is that whereby He was equally obedient unto death for the expiation of our sins, for which eternal death was due. For the apostle understood that it is by way of both parts of this obedience that we are justified in the sight of God and eternally saved.

18. The consequence of obedience unto death is the remission of our sins and, as a result, complete liberation from eternal death. Even so, in the same way the consequence of His perfect obedience in fulfilling the law is possession of eternal life. For both parts of His obedience, which are supplied by Christ in a real way, are communicated to us by way of imputation and truly become ours by right of union when the whole Christ—regardless of how great He is—is made one flesh with us and we, in turn, with Him.

19. With respect to this same imputation, the apostolic writings declare far and wide that we (as members) with the one Christ (as with a head) are now crucified, are dead, are buried, are raised from the dead, are ascended into heaven, are seated with Him in the highest heavens, and, finally, as the apostle says, are blessed in that same Christ with every spiritual blessing [Eph. 1:3; 2:5–6]. And, truly, it is not merely on account of hope that we are reputed thus but rather because in Christ our Head that is what we are right now in heaven before God.

20. That statement of the apostle pertains to the same point: "Christ became wisdom, righteousness, sanctification, and redemption for us" [1 Cor. 1[:30]). And this fits harmoniously with Jeremiah's saying: "Jehovah (namely, Christ), is our righteousness" [Jer. 23:6].

21. Finally, in the plainest way possible, the Scriptures teach that in addition to other blessings we obtain two things by way of faith in Christ. First, that our sins and all of our unrighteousness are not imputed to us and, therefore, that we are freed from the guilt of eternal death. Second, and conversely, that the righteousness of Christ is imputed to us. That is, that on account of Christ's righteousness, laid hold of and made ours by faith, we are reputed righteous before God and reckoned worthy of eternal life.

22. To this pertains the word *imputing*, which Paul often employs when he has justification in mind, saying that sin is not imputed to those who believe in Christ but rather that their faith is imputed as righteousness (Rom. 4:5ff.).

23. But what does the apostle mean by the word *faith*? Certainly not the very action of our faith on its own, for even that is also our work. Yet he denies that we are justified by our works. Rather, the apostle means that faith is that which lays hold of the thing itself, that is, Christ's very own righteousness, or Christ Himself, who is our righteousness, as also Jeremiah preached, "Jehovah our righteousness" [Jer. 23:6].

24. Thus, two things necessarily coincide for the justification of our life, namely, the forgiveness of our unrighteousness (or the remission of our sins) and the imputation of an alien righteousness, that is, Christ's laid hold of by[10] faith. Indeed, the remission of our sins, namely, that we not be condemned to eternal death, but the imputation of Christ's righteousness, namely, that we might be reckoned worthy of eternal life.

25. For true and Christian justification, which the apostle calls "justification of life" [Rom. 5:18], consists in these: namely, remission of sins, and so liberation from eternal death, *as well as* in the free imputation of fully perfect righteousness (which is Christ's alone), and so the judgment of eternal life. Take note of the word *life* because we are not only freed from death but are also justified unto life.

26. From this it is manifest that in the Sacred Scriptures the word *imputing* signifies both parts of complete justification by way of synecdoche,[11] because the one without the other cannot stand. Indeed, there is no remission of our sins without the imputation of Christ's righteousness, no imputation of righteousness without the free remission of sins, so that both absolution from the guilt of eternal death and, in turn, the assertion of inheritance of eternal life may be had together.

And let this suffice concerning the first manner[12] whereby all of

---

10. *per.*

11. συνεκδοχικῶς.

12. *modo.*

Christ's treasures, and especially His righteousness, are communicated to us, namely, by way of imputation.

*The Real Communication of Blessings*
1. Moreover, concerning the second manner,[13] namely, by real communication, there exists nearly an infinite number of testimonies in the Scriptures, so a tedious demonstration would not be useful. For example, there is that saying of John, "He gives the Spirit to Jesus without measure" [John 3:34], and, "of His fullness we have all received" [1:16]. Again, "He who does righteousness is righteous" [1 John 3:7], for John speaks of inherent righteousness. To this also pertains the saying, "Let he who is righteous be righteous still" [Rev. 22:11], for he receives this righteousness incrementally. Again, the saying to the Philippians, "I pray that your love may yet abound more…," and that you may press on, "filled with the fruits of righteousness" [Phil. 1:9, 11].

2. For Christ our Bridegroom, therefore, communicates this inherent righteousness to us so that it may perpetually bring forth righteous fruits in us and in our neighbors.

3. To these is added another inestimable gift. For the Lord Jesus accomplishes His grace toward us so that whatever we do from this inherent righteousness, although it is imperfectly done and contaminated by the filth of our flesh, nevertheless, it is pleasing and acceptable to God, all of our blemishes being covered over by the cloak of Christ's own mercy and righteousness. This accords with that saying, "Blessed are they whose sins are covered" [Ps. 32:1]. And, "There is no damnation for those who are in Christ Jesus, who walk not according to the flesh but according to the Spirit" [Rom. 8:1].

4. On the contrary, He deigns to reward those imperfect works of the bride with many great gifts, according to the apostle's saying, "Godliness has promises for the present life and for the life to come as well" [1 Tim. 4:8].

5. But insofar as the innate defect of nature (or indwelling sin) from Adam remains in our flesh until the end of our life (and that according

---

13. *modo.*

to our Bridegroom's provision for each one of us for our humbling, and for perpetual battle, and for the increasing of our faith), not only does He not impute it in order to condemn us, but rather, by the power of His Spirit communicated to us, He little by little and day by day reduces, diminishes, weakens, removes, and finally extinguishes it altogether.

6. To this pertains what the apostle says, Christ washes and sanctifies His church until, at last, He might present her glorious in the sight of God, having neither spot nor wrinkle (Eph. 5[:26–27]).

7. Nor does Christ do this merely according to His grace. Rather, He also causes a holy and perpetual desire to be *in us*, in order that this might be completed as soon as possible, so that we might finally be brought through to His state, wherein we are no longer able to sin. And this pertains to that saying of the apostle: "O wretched man that I am, who will free me from this body of death?" (Rom. 7[:24]). And that to the Philippians: "I desire to be loosed and to be with Christ" (Phil. 1[:23]). And that word of the bride to her Bridegroom: "Come, Lord Jesus! Come!" (Rev. 22[:17, 20]). And, finally, that which we pray in the Lord's Prayer every day, saying, "May Your kingdom come" (Matt. 6[:10]). Again, "Free us from evil" [v. 13].

8. But what does this mean, except that Christ gives the church and every one of the faithful the gift of perseverance in the faith and love of Christ? To this pertains that saying of the apostle: "Who will separate me from the love of God, which is in Christ Jesus our Lord?" (Rom. 8[:39]).

And let these suffice concerning the blessings that are really communicated to us from the treasures of Christ for leading a spiritual and truly happy life in this age. Who could describe how great, how many, and how precious they are?

*The Various Spiritual Gifts*[14] *of Christ*
1. In Christ's human nature there are so many other gifts of the Holy Spirit as well, given without measure, which are not so necessary for promoting the salvation of each one of the faithful, such as the gift of

---

14. χαρίσματα.

prophecy, of tongues, of performing miracles, of healing, and others, concerning which there is more than enough in the Holy Scriptures.

2. Moreover, the Bridegroom-Christ does not refuse these to the bride-church, albeit, they are neither always nor equally imparted to each and every one of the faithful, but only to whom He wills, when He wills, and as much as He wills, because no other way of imparting gifts is expedient for the church. Concerning the variety of gifts, the apostle speaks in 1 Corinthians 12: "To each one is given a disclosure by the Spirit for profit," and "The one and the same Spirit does these things, distributing individually to each one as He wills" [vv. 7, 11].

3. For in carnal marriage, likewise, it is neither profitable nor advantageous for all that the bridegroom has stored up always to be imparted to the wife, but rather only those things that are necessary for her salvation, honor, and consolation. And it should be sufficient for the bride to know that whenever she is in need, all things will also be imparted to her. For this is just the same as if she did actually and always possess them.

4. But of what kind, I ask, and how great is the treasure of blessings pertaining to the life of this present age—not merely human life, but also spiritual and Christian—which are not only imputed by Christ but also are communicated by a real superintendence? What are they? They are such that He transforms even every evil that befalls us in this age into a greater good, as the apostle testifies: "For those who love God, all things cooperate for good" (Rom. 8[:28]).

Take Joseph and Christ as examples for us (and let us leave all the others unmentioned). What, how great, what types, and how many injuries did Joseph suffer—as much from his own family as from outsiders—and all on account of his piety and because he was claiming to be singularly beloved by God? He was mocked on account of prophetic dreams, thrown into a well, sold to strangers, taken into Egypt, locked in a jail—but to what end? By the singular favor of God, all these things yielded to his ultimate dignity and glory. And concerning Himself, Christ says, "The Christ ought to suffer and thus enter into His glory" [Luke 24:26]. And, as Paul writes, "He humbled Himself, becoming obedient unto death, even the death of the cross, for which reason also God exalted Him, and gave Him the name that is above every name, that at the name of Jesus every knee should bow" [Phil. 2:8–10]. Finally, as the whole church celebrates, He suffered, died, and was buried, and He rose again, ascended into heaven, and sits at the right hand of the Father.

5. Indeed, even in the very suffering of calamities, persecutions, tortures, and, finally, death itself, He is always with us by the power of His Spirit; He strengthens us and bestows great and extraordinary comfort. He does this not only to prevent us from succumbing to those trials but also so that we might declare victory in battle as conquerors in the end.

6. That passage in 2 Corinthians 4 is appropriate here: "We are afflicted in all things, but we are not crushed; we are perplexed, but not driven to despair. We suffer persecution, but we are not forsaken…and we are not destroyed" [vv. 8–9]. Again, 1 Corinthians 10: "God is faithful; He will not let you be tempted beyond what you are able to endure, but He will make a way out with the temptation," indeed, a happy way [v. 13]. Again, Romans 5: "Not only this but let us also glory in tribulations, knowing that tribulation works patience" [v. 3]. Again, Acts 5: "The apostles left the presence of the council, rejoicing that they had been considered worthy to suffer abuse for the name of Jesus" [v. 41].

7. For daily, more and more, by means of all those evils troubling our flesh, He mortifies and purges all the remnants of sin that remain in us, as by the very best medical purgatives, even to the end of the world.

8. Finally, if calamities are inflicted upon us on account of our sins, let this be for our correction, that we may not be condemned with this world, as the apostle teaches in 1 Corinthians 11[:32]. Moreover, if on Christ's account and on account of our holy marriage to Him, we are conformed to our Bridegroom's image and carry His mark, then it is a sign of His special kindness toward us. And what bride would not freely bear the mark of her princely or royal bridegroom, when doing so would greatly increase her own dignity and glory?

## The Blessings of the Age to Come

1. But what shall I say concerning the blessings that pertain to the eternal and blessed life of the next age? Surely, it is altogether necessary that the Bridegroom's own palace, together with all of its furniture, decorations,

and splendor—indeed, with all of its halls and its servants—becomes the bride's common property. For this is the will of the Bridegroom, as the Bridegroom Himself testified, saying, "I desire that where I am, they (meaning those faithful ones that constitute the church, Christ's bride) may also be" (John 17[:24]). Again, "I will return to you and I will take you to Myself." Again, "I go to prepare a place for you" (14[:3]).

2. But the apostle says that the quantity and quality of the blessings that await us there cannot possibly be explained: "Eye has not seen nor ear heard, nor has entered into the heart of man, what things God has prepared for those who love Him" (1 Cor. 2[:9]). But we who are made one flesh with Christ know for certain that we will see those blessings and that, by the force of this holy marriage, we will possess them eternally, according to the saying of Christ: "Come, you who are blessed of My Father, inherit the kingdom prepared for you from the foundation of the world" (Matt. 25[:34]).

Wherefore, let all of us, together with holy Job, say out of true faith, "I know that my Redeemer lives and that on the last day I will rise from the earth, and I will see God in my flesh, my Savior, whom I will see, I myself and not another, and my eyes will behold. This, my hope, is laid up in my bosom" (Job 19[:25–27]). And with the whole church, Christ's bride, let us cry out to the Bridegroom, sighing and groaning with our whole heart, "Come, Lord Jesus. Come" (Rev. 22[:17, 20]), and, on account of Your great love toward us, receive us into Your Father's heavenly house. To Whom be honor, praise, and glory. Amen.

# Bibliography

Almond, Philip C. *Adam and Eve in Seventeenth-Century Thought*. Cambridge: Cambridge University Press, 1999.

Aquinas, Thomas. *Summa Theologica*. Translated by Fathers of the English Dominican Province. 5 vols. Notre Dame, Ind.: Christian Classics, 1981.

Archer, Ian W. "Palavicino, Sir Horatio (c. 1540–1600)." In *Oxford Dictionary of National Biography*. Oxford University Press, 2004; online ed. https://doi.org/10.1093/ref:odnb/21153.

Augustine of Hippo. *Expositions of the Psalms*. Translated by Maria Boulding. Edited by John E. Rotelle and Boniface Ramsey. 6 vols. The Works of Saint Augustine III/15–20. Hyde Park, N.Y.: New City, 2000–2004.

———. *Homilies on the Gospel of John*. Translated by Edmund Hill. Edited by Allan D. Fitzgerald. 2 vols. The Works of Saint Augustine I/12–13. Hyde Park, N.Y.: New City, 2009–2020.

———. *Letters*. Translated by Roland Teske. Edited by John E. Rotelle and Boniface Ramsey. 4 vols. The Works of Saint Augustine II/1–4. Hyde Park, N.Y.: New City, 2001–2005.

Austin, Kenneth. *From Judaism to Calvinism: The Life and Writings of Immanuel Tremellius (c. 1510–1580)*. St. Andrews Studies in Reformation History. Aldershot, U.K.: Ashgate, 2007.

Bullinger, Heinrich. *Bullingers Korrespondenz mit den Graubündern*. Edited by Traugott Schiess. 3 vols. Basel: Basler Buch und Antiquariatshandlung, 1904–1906.

Burchill, Christopher J. "Girolamo Zanchi in Strasburg 1553–1563." PhD diss., Cambridge University, 1980.

———. "Girolamo Zanchi: Portrait of a Reformed Theologian and His Work." *Sixteenth Century Journal* 15 (1984): 185–207.

Chrysostom, John. *Argumentum Epistolae primae ad Corinthios, et Homiliae XLIV in eadem Epistolam.* Vol. 10 of *Joannis Chyrsostomi Opera omnia.* 2nd ed. Edited by Theobald Fix. Paris: Gaume, 1837.

Cyril of Alexandria. *Commentary on John.* Translated by David Maxwell. Edited by Joel C. Elowsky. 2 vols. Ancient Christian Texts. Downers Grove, Ill.: IVP Academic, 2013–2015.

Donnelly, John Patrick. "A Sixteenth Century Case of Publish or Perish/Parish." *Sixteenth Century Journal* 6 (1975): 112–13.

Farmer, Craig S. "Introduction to John 1–12." In *John 1–12*, edited by Craig S. Farmer, xlv–lx. Vol. 4 of *Reformation Commentary on Scripture*, edited by Timothy George and Scott M. Manetsch. New Testament. Downers Grove, Ill.: IVP Academic, 2014.

Farthing, John L. "*De coniugio spirituali*: Jerome Zanchi on Eph. 5:22–33." *Sixteenth Century Journal* 24 (1993): 621–52.

Fesko, J. V. *Beyond Calvin: Union with Christ and Justification in Early Modern Reformed Theology (1517–1700).* Reformed Historical Theology 20. Göttingen: Vandenhoeck & Ruprecht, 2012.

———. "Girolamo Zanchi on Union with Christ and the Final Judgment." *Perichoresis* 18 (2020): 41–56.

———. "Jerome Zanchi on Union with Christ and Justification." *Puritan Reformed Journal* 2 (2010): 55–78.

Gerhard, Johann. *Loci theologici.* 9 vols. Frankfurt and Hamburg, 1657.

Gründler, Otto. "Thomism and Calvinism in the Theology of Girolamo Zanchi (1516–1590)." ThD diss., Princeton Theological Seminary, 1961.

Hilary of Poitiers. *The Trinity.* Translated by Stephen McKenna. The Fathers of the Church 25. Washington, D.C.: Catholic University of America Press, 1954.

Hondius, Hendrik. *Icones virorum nostra patrumque memoria illustrium.* The Hague, 1599.

Jerome. "To Pammachius against John of Jerusalem." In *NPNF2*, 6:424–47.

Kidder, Richard. *A Commentary on the Five Books of Moses.* 2 vols. London, 1694.

Leo I. "Letter 59: To the Clergy and People of the City of Constantinople." In *NPNF2*, 12:59–61.

Lewis, C. S. Introduction to *On the Incarnation: The Treatise* De Incarnatione Verbi Dei, by Athanasius, 3–10. Crestwood, N.Y.: St. Vladimir's Seminary Press, 1996.

Lindholm, Stefan. *Jerome Zanchi (1516–90) and the Analysis of Reformed Scholastic Christology.* Göttingen: Vandenhoeck & Ruprecht, 2016.

Luther, Martin. *Standard Edition of Luther's Works.* 31 vols. Minneapolis: Lutherans in All Lands, 1903–1910.

McGinn, Bernard, ed. *The Essential Writings of Christian Mysticism.* New York: Modern Library, 2006.

Merkle, Benjamin. *Defending the Trinity in the Reformed Palatinate: The Elohistae.* Oxford Theology and Religion Monographs. Oxford: Oxford University Press, 2015.

Muddiman, John. *A Commentary on the Epistle to the Ephesians.* Black's New Testament Commentaries. London: Continuum, 2001.

O'Banion, Patrick J. "Jerome Zanchi, the Application of Theology, and the Rise of the English Practical Divinity Tradition." *Renaissance and Reformation,* n.s., 29 (2005): 97–120.

Oecolampadius, Johannes. *In Genesim enarratio.* Basel, 1536.

Pearse, Edward. *The Best Match: or, the Soul's Espousal to Christ.* 1673. Reprint, London: Thomas and Ward, 1839.

Robinson, Hastings, ed. *The Zurich Letters.* 2nd series. Cambridge: Cambridge University Press, 1845.

Schmidt, Charles. "Girolamo Zanchi." *Theologische Studien und Kritiken* 32 (1859): 625–708.

Selderhuis, Herman J. "Introduction to the Psalms." In *Psalms 1–72,* edited by Herman J. Selderhuis, xlv–lvii. Vol. 7 of *Reformation Commentary on Scripture,* edited by Timothy George and Scott M. Manetsch. Old Testament. Downers Grove, Ill.: IVP Academic, 2015.

Steinmetz, David C. "The Superiority of Pre-Critical Exegesis." *Theology Today* 37 (1980): 27–38.

Tamburello, Dennis E. *Union with Christ: John Calvin and the Mysticism of St. Bernard.* Louisville: Westminster John Knox, 1994.

Tertullian. *Adversus Marcionem: Books 1–3.* Edited and translated by Edward Evans. Oxford Early Christian Texts. Oxford: Clarendon, 1972.

Tremellius, Immanuel. *In Hoseam prophetam interpretatio et enarratio.* Lyon, 1563.

Tremellius, Immanuel, and Franciscus Junius. *Testamenti Veteris Biblia Sacra.* 5 vols. London, 1581.

Tylenda, Joseph. "Girolamo Zanchi and John Calvin: A Study in Discipleship as Seen through Their Correspondence." *Calvin Theological Journal* 10 (1975): 101–41.

Velde, Dolf te. *The Doctrine of God in Reformed Orthodoxy, Karl Barth, and the Utrecht School.* Studies in Reformed Theology 25. Leiden: Brill, 2013.

Vermigli, Peter Martyr. *In primum librum Mosis.* Zurich, 1569.

Vischer, Lukas. "Girolamo Zanchi, reformierter Prediger in Chiavenna." *Bündnerische Monatsblätter* 10 (1951): 289–301.

Walker, George. *God Made Visible in His Works, or, a Treatise of the External Works of God.* London, 1641.

Zanchi, Girolamo. *De religione christiana fides – Confession of the Christian Religion.* Edited by Luca Baschera and Christian Moser. 2 vols. Studies in the History of Christian Traditions 135. Leiden: Brill, 2007.

————. *De spirituali inter Christum et ecclesiam, singulosque fideles connubio.* Herborn, 1591.

————. *De tribus Elohim, sive de uno vero Deo aeterno, Patre, Filio et Spiritu Sancto, uno eodemque Iehova.* Frankfurt, 1572.

————. *In Hoseam commentarium.* Neustadt, 1600.

————. *Speculum Christianum, or, a Christian Survey of the Conscience.* Edited and translated by Henry Nelson. London, 1614.

# Index